BECOMING MARIA

Love and Chaos in the South Bronx

BECOMING MARIA

Love and Chaos in the South Bronx

SONIA MANZANO

Scholastic Press / New York

All rights reserved. Published by Scholastic Press, an imprint of Scholastic Inc.,
Publishers since 1920. SCHOLASTIC, SCHOLASTIC PRESS, and associated logos are
trademarks and/or registered trademarks of Scholastic Inc.

The publisher does not have any control over and does not assume any responsibility for
author or third-party websites or their content.

Library of Congress Cataloging-in-Publication Data Available

ISBN 978-0-545-62184-7

10 9 8 7 6 5 4   18 19

Printed in the U.S.A.   23
First edition, September 2015

Book design by Elizabeth B. Parisi

To my mother, Isidra Rivera Manzano,
and my brother Enrique Manzano

CONTENTS

SONIA MANZANO
Drama
Wardrobe Mistress
Journalism
Playwriting

PART I

Fragments

CHAPTER 1

Kid Diaper Meets Mystery Girl

M y mother is cooking my father. He is trapped, immobilized, with his knees pressed up against his chin in the kitchen tub as she moves back and forth from a nearby stove pouring hot water over his soapy head. A dark little girl comes into the room and they send her away.

Some days or nights later I hear a symphony of yelling and screaming and body shoves and slaps. When I crawl into the kitchen the door opens and the little girl enters between two big white policemen. My father tries to get un-drunk by standing tightly; my mother tries smiling.

"No *problema*, officer," says my father.

"*Todo bien*," adds my mother, turning away so the cop won't see the mark on her face. She wipes down the metal panel top of the tub she had cooked my father in, like their fight was nothing special. Once the policemen are gone my mother and father yell at the little girl, whoever she is. From then on out it seems she is sometimes there and sometimes not.

She is *not* there on the night my grandmother, livid about something, punches a wall and my finger gets caught in a door in the confusion. "*Duele, duele*," I cry, telling Ma that it hurt, and she makes it all better with her magic warm breath—but I still look for the little girl. How should I know where she is? I'm still in diapers.

We move to the Bronx and before I can turn around the little girl is in our new place standing against the far wall between windows that face the street. She is wearing dark dungarees, a black T-shirt, and a skullcap pulled down to her eyebrows. The hair sticking out from under is thick. I want to get a better look but feel shy—besides, the light is coming into my eyes.

"It's not *pelo malo*," I hear a neighbor woman whispering to Ma in the kitchen.

"No," says Ma. "Not bad hair at all. Just that my aunt, who I left her with in Puerto Rico, washed it with detergent. What can you do? They lived in El Fanguito."

"Oh . . . *terrible* . . . what a terrible place to have to live. God knows how many babies drowned in the rivers of shit that flowed under the houses," the neighbor answers.

They have a moment of silence for all the dead babies, then the neighbor goes on, "So washing her hair in detergent was what made it kinky; it's not that she's . . ."

She stops talking again. I wait for more but only hear heavy silence.

They come into the living room. The neighbor is tall and thin and looks like she smells something bad. My mother holds a hairbrush like a weapon.

"Aurea, *ven acá*."

Ah! Some information. The little girl's name is Aurea!

"Come, I'll fix your hair," Ma says. But Aurea turns away angrily. She is always angry.

I am walking through a dark, wet room.

"This way," says Pops.

"I can't see," says Ma, and then adds, alarmed, "Sonia, don't go near the wall!"

I jump back just in time. The walls are dripping with water. Was it raining inside? It smells funny down here, too—like the sidewalk, but here there is a thin layer of dirt on the ground as well. I know because I keep kicking it up as Ma drags me farther and farther toward a yellow light in the distance. We pass a big round machine that shimmers and shakes and burps and coughs heat, and continue dodging the cement columns holding up the building above us until we reach another door that Pops pushes open.

"This way," he says again.

"*Ay, Dios mío,*" moans Ma.

It's a space for people to live in with a bed and table and chairs, but the room is not much different from the basement we just crept through. A man and a woman with hollow eyes look up at us as we enter. There are two little boys about my size wrestling in the corner. One isn't wearing pants and I stare at something tiny and dangling between his legs. He has snot hanging out of his nose that stops at his upper lip. There is a girl a few years older whose coughing fits whip around her stringy hair. She stares at me between hacks as the grown-ups greet and talk. Suddenly Ma screams.

"Oh my God."

The little boy with the dangling thing is taking a poop on the table. The woman giggles and the man yells, "Mickey, what the hell are you doing?" Ma picks me up. By the time they find something to clean up his mess he is done dumping. I can feel Ma's anger through her dress. She keeps saying, *"AveMaríaPurísima,* there are bathrooms here!" as she paces up and down the tiny space.

"Don't worry, Franco," says Pops. "There might be a real apartment available on Fulton Avenue later. For now just live here and *búscate la vida."*

"Look for your life"? My father had just told him to "look for his life." What does that mean?

"Sí, seguro. I'm ready to work and make money right away," says Franco.

"You'll come with me tomorrow. I got a roofing job you can help with."

"Okay!"

"And what about me?" says the woman. "I can sew a little."

"There's piecework all over the city you can do, Iris," says Ma irritably. "We'll find something for you tomorrow . . ."

I can tell Ma wants to get out of there so after a short while we say good-bye. Out in the street Ma says *"Terrible, terrible,"* over and over again.

"All I could find for them," says Pops. "They weren't supposed to come so quick. I just told your brother Franco two weeks ago he should *think* about coming to New York. How could I know he was just going to show up so quickly? Did you want him to move in with *us?* I didn't think he was going to get airline tickets and come right away." He stops for a minute before saying, "Things must be worse in Puerto Rico than I thought."

Those two words, *Puerto Rico,* make me listen for more, but there is no more coming. Ma keeps quiet as we trudge up Third Avenue as I hear the train rumbling into the station above my head.

"Franco is *your* brother," says Pops, rubbing it in.

My mother's words jump him. "And your sister, La Boba, got scared and started screaming when I tried to get her to step onto the escalator at Gimbels last week. I was so embarrassed . . ."

"Aw, come on, you know how she is . . ."

I want to know "how she is" and why my father's sister is called "the dumb one" when she is sweet and nice and looks at me with Chinese eyes and I can understand her even though her tongue is thick and sloppy in her mouth.

My parents snap and growl about *her* brother Franco, and *his* sister, La Boba, all the way up the stairs to our apartment. The people who live in the dungeon are my uncle Frank; his wife, Iris; and my cousins Mickey, Chaty, and Mimi, who have just come from that strange place, Puerto Rico. We see them almost as often as we see Ma's other brother, Uncle Eddie; his wife, Bon Bon; her daughter, Zoraida; and their son, Little Eddie, who is already my favorite. I don't think my father is too happy about Ma having loving brothers even though he's friendly with them.

Aurea and I are alone and my father comes home wildly drunk. "Isa!" he screams. My mother is not here to answer him because she is not home. He doesn't notice us, doesn't ask Aurea where my mother might be, though she is old enough to answer. After my father runs and peeks into all four rooms, plus the kitchen, it finally dawns on him that she is not home! He comes back into the living room and looks about ferociously. Does he think Ma is hiding under the sofa, or behind the picture of Jesus Christ on the wall? Maybe she's curled up in the ashtray. I think Aurea has gone to hide.

When he finally understands that his target is not home he picks up the coffee table and sends it flying through the air. I watch it smack into the wall and splinter. Then he picks up a lamp and sends *it* flying into the door of their bedroom, and I watch the lightbulb shatter like my feelings even though I'm not sure what I'm feeling except that I am beyond scared and turn into a one-note, catatonic, unbroken scream.

My father stops and looks around, wondering where that high-pitched squeal is coming from, and notices me stuck in my spot, the top of my head just reaching his knees. His red eyes refocus like a robot villain's. *Who is this kid,* he seems to think, *and how did she get here?* My screeching bothers him because he crouches down and comforts me, pawing me on the head with his big-callused, hard hand. But I don't know if it's safe to accept the comforting, though the whiskey smell coming from him is so sweet, I like it. But just when I'm comforted down to simple whimpering and sucking in great gusts of air, the devil that's riding him takes over and he forgets about me, stands up, takes the mirror off the wall with the painted pink flamingoes on it and sends it flying onto the radiator. My whimpering ratchets up to the one-pitch scream again as he kicks in the television set before running out of the apartment.

I run to our fourth-floor window, looking out for anything, when I see Uncle Eddie's car pull up. Out spills his wife, Bon Bon; my uncle Frank; his wife, Iris; and my beautiful mother. She is dressed in a soft-colored yellow dress with pleats down the front that she made herself. My father enters my line of vision as he lunges for her. Her brothers restrain him, and I can tell even from the fourth floor that Ma would rip his face off if she could.

There is something beautiful in the picture they make jerking around in the streetlight. And when the Third Avenue El comes swishing through, right in front of our window so suddenly, I feel like I am in the center of the universe and I am happy that they have had this fight because it has introduced me to the wonderful window. And that's where I go every day, all the time between assaults when there is nervous calm.

From there I spy on the neighbors: sexy Flor with her big ass and yellow cotton-candy hair, and mean Genoveva, who always looks like she is smelling something bad, and pretty, Americanized Lydia, who wears her hair in a flip, and La Puerca/Bizca, who has two names because she is both a dirty pig—La Puerca—and cross-eyed—Bizca—and the big-headed red-haired Cabeza family. They all go in and out of Don Joe's bodega right next to our building, unaware that I am watching them and that I know what they buy and how much time they spend hanging around talking.

I also spy on the Third Avenue elevated train barreling into our neighborhood every few minutes so I see the people spill out of the cars and scatter down the stairs of the station like marbles down a flight of steps—careening past the shoeshine boys, shooting up toward Crotona Park where Chaty and Mickey play so hard Ma feels sorry for the trees, or roll on down toward Bathgate Avenue, where they can buy live chickens from Jewish people who chop the chickens' heads off and hang them upside down to bleed.

But mostly I wait for Ma to come home from work. Any train could be hers, and suddenly she appears like magic and waves and smiles at me in such a way I know I am the most beloved girl in the world. I'm so happy I tremble, watching her disappear under the station awning then reappear, going down the steps, past the enviable shoeshine boys who are outside all day.

And she doesn't go up to Fulton or down to Bathgate like the other marbles but straight onto Third Avenue and to me. She walks under the stripes of light the sun makes through the tracks and once she gets past Don Joe's bodega I know exactly how long it'll take her to get to our door.

"Mami!" She is so pretty with her little waist and high-heeled shoes.

"*Ya, ya, ya.*" She hugs me, laughing and kissing me all over my head and neck. I search for the half-eaten candy bar that is always in her purse, but by the time I turn back to her the moment I have waited for all day is over, and suddenly feeling denied and drained I go back to the window and wait for the second and last part of the day to begin.

My father comes home and I listen for trouble but know we'll be safe when I hear him playing the guitar, singing loudly.

"*Mamá, yo quiero saber, de dónde son los cantantes . . .*" he croons until he suddenly barks, "Sonia, scratch my back." Dragging myself away from the window I climb up and stand behind him as he sits on the sofa and I scratch his back that seems acres big. Methodically I work my way between his shoulders, then down the sides, then along the top of his belt before filling in its vastness with general scraping. I peek at the movie on the television. King Kong is hanging on to the Empire State Building as planes attack, and I feel so sad about it I stop scratching. My father wiggles his ears. I laugh. He does it again, making me laugh harder. I wish I could wiggle my ears like him and I try, concentrating and concentrating, but it's impossible, I can only feel my ears with my hands; still, I wish we could wiggle and laugh together forever. But he gets bored in an instant and thinks of something else.

"*¡Agua!*" he says.

I look at his face but his eyes say he is somewhere else. I slip off the sofa and run into the kitchen, where my mother is standing at the stove.

"*Papi quiere...*"

I don't have to finish because she knows what I want and fills a glass of water for me to give to him. I reach for the glass, and though her hands are free, she points with her lips to newly fried pork rinds she has rendered dry for flavoring, and offers me the crispy tidbit leftovers. She looks like an angel to me as I chew on the salty treat.

"*Que los encuentro galantes...*" My father has begun to sing again.

"*¡Ven a comer!*" Ma calls Pops to eat. Entering, he grabs the glass of water out of her hands and gulps it as he sits. When he's done eating Ma calls to me and Aurea, who watches my father suspiciously as he leaves. I sit and play with my food.

"*Eat,*" Ma threatens.

"She don't want to eat," says Aurea.

"She's going to eat or else," says Ma.

After a while Aurea goes to her room and I rest my head on the table so I can play with my food from that angle because it looks like it could be more fun.

"You are not leaving this table until you finish," scolds Ma, standing and eating at the stove. But she gets tired after a while. "Oh, never mind," she says, picking up my plate. "Good food going to waste. *Terrible.*"

Yay! I'm free! Running to the door I am just in time to see the super picking up the garbage. He stops on every floor with a large garbage can collecting people's trash, which he empties into his larger can, then packs it down by jumping into it with both feet. Food smacks against the building's walls and I know that our neighbors had the same thing for dinner that we had—some sort of rice and beans. I wish I could jump in the garbage like that.

"*A dormir* . . ." Ma drags me away from the door, triple-locks it, and shoos me into the bedroom.

"*¡Avanza!*" says Ma, pointing to the chamber pot. A gloominess falls over us. She hates that I wet the bed—and I really feel bad about it, too. She waits until I start to pee in the pot, then leaves to do something else. The sound of the El coming into the station drowns out the sound I make peeing.

Getting into bed I examine my feet. Manipulating them with my hands I discover a curious parallel relationship between my feet and my hands. A certain symmetry emerges . . . I begin to hyperventilate . . . because . . . I thought . . . that—yes . . . it must be right . . . I have the same number of fingers as I have toes! Is that possible? I count again—this time firmly separating each toe from the previous one to keep them from dangling together at the end of my foot like a bunch of grapes. I count again, and again, and realize that I do indeed have ten toes just like I have ten fingers. I call out, "Ma, I have ten toes!"

She reenters the room and then a look of disbelief momentarily rearranges her face.

"Go to sleep," she says, leaving.

Her command that I should go to sleep does not even bother me. The symmetry of my digits at the ends of my arms and legs both excites and calms me. It proves there is order in the universe. I snuggle in and stare at the ceiling, where I find shapes in the cracked plaster. I see a boat, a house, a cloud . . .

CHAPTER 2

Family Beatings

*B*orracho! ¡*Madre de Dios!*" Doña Cabeza's voice wakes me up. What is she doing in our apartment so early? I get up and see her and Flor clucking around my mother's bed. Peeking between them I see Ma's angry face. She has a bump on her head, a black eye, and bruises on her arms.

"Goddamn him," Ma spits out.

"Eat the soup," commands Doña Cabeza.

I want to see if I can tell if it is pigeon broth. Doña Cabeza's sons raise pigeons on the roof and she often breaks their necks and cooks them, but I can't see because her big head of red hair is in the way. Her family's name is perfect—"Cabeza," it means *head* in Spanish— and Doña Cabeza and the five sons she lords over have the biggest heads, all covered in thick, flaming-red hair.

"*No, gracias,*" says my mother, turning down the soup. "I can't even eat."

"That's how men are," offers Flor, the words lisping out of her mouth because of her missing teeth. I look at the hole of her mouth surrounded by red lips and her cotton-candy pale yellow hair. She lives with her two children and manages to keep two brothers, who fight over her, at bay. "That's why I stay single."

They all nod in agreement.

"*¡Borracho!* And he hit your head against the radiator? Horrible."

What? My father was drunk? He hit her head against the radiator!

"*Pobrecita.*"

Can that be true? I can't believe it! They repeat the story over and over again.

"Drunk?"

"*¡Madre de Dios!*"

"*Terrible.*"

Flor and Doña Cabeza eventually leave, agreeing on their way out that this happened because my father loves my mother so much. My mother and I, finally alone, look at each other. She yawns, then suddenly jumps out of bed, goes into the kitchen, and pulls some cheese out of the refrigerator. Then she opens a great big green tin of crackers.

"Want some?"

"Yes," I say.

There's a knock on the door and she quickly puts the cheese and crackers back.

"But . . . ?"

"Later! Go answer the door."

I go to answer the door.

"Wait!"

I stop and watch her get back into bed and arrange her face to look sad again.

"Now!"

"Who?" I ask carefully like I've been taught to do.

"Genoveva," says one voice.

"Lydia," says another.

I hate Genoveva but I like Lydia because she is pretty and white and so Americanized she speaks perfect English and is always so nice to her son, Dennis, even when he nods himself to sleep on the sidewalk. The door has a police lock; it's heavy, but I feel I can do it. I must.

Genoveva and Lydia flutter passed me, like I'm not even there and didn't just go through all the trouble of opening the door, so I hurry up and stand between them and my mother so they see me. But I must be invisible because they look through me and gasp at the sight of Ma. Genoveva has an ice bag and is happy to have someone to minister to. My mother begins her sorry tale all over again.

"He was like a crazy man. So drunk . . ." says Ma.

"Jesus, Mary, and Joseph . . ." says pinched-face Genoveva.

"And look at all the broken furniture," says Lydia.

Then they look at my broken mother, taking in her bump and black eye.

"Here, put this ice on that bump," says Genoveva.

"I have makeup that can cover that eye so you can go to work," says Lydia.

"Wear long sleeves for work," suggests Genoveva.

Then, out of nowhere, comes the big question. "Why did he do it?"

I try to think—is it because he loves her? Right?

They go on.

"Men!"

"Men," Lydia agrees.

Men? What does that mean? Some men? All men? Do all men bang their wives' heads into radiators and punch them? My cousin

Little Eddie is going to be a man someday—will he beat his wife as well?

There is another knock. "Who?" I ask cautiously, opening the door a sliver.

"*¿Quién es?*" My mom wants to know who it is. I run back and tell her.

"It's La Puerca/Bizca."

Genoveva and Lydia snicker.

"Shhh. Don't call her that!" says Ma.

"It's not her fault," says Lydia, defending me. "Everybody calls her that!"

"Not to her face," says my mother. "Let her in!"

I let her in and look to Ma. She always laughs at this woman but now she is serious. The story is told again.

"This radiator?"

On cue I point to the radiator.

"*¡Madre de Dios!*"

"*¡Terrible! ¡Pobrecita!*"

I nod in agreement and sigh like Lydia did and I go along with the script. All the women's words fly around in my head.

"Never let him into the apartment again. You must think of yourself and the children. No man is worth it—even if he loves you. Don't let him treat you like that. Men."

Everyone knows how others should live, and I wonder if everyone's life is like a coat they can give each other to try on for size. Or were the neighbors part of our lives, like waves sneaking up and then away on sandy shores?

"Is there somewhere you could run away to?" asks Genoveva.

"It'll be hard at first, but you work! You make money!" adds Lydia. "You could do it! You make your own money!"

"I'll do it," says Ma forcefully.

It's decided that we go to Uncle Eddie's house in Bethpage. I'm thrilled to be with Cousin Eddie and forget all about my mother's bruises. When we arrive at my uncle's house, Little Eddie and I lock hearts and souls. Above our heads the grown-ups whisper and plot about what to do, but Eddie and I don't care because his shiny red tricycle with banners at the handles is the most beautiful thing in the world. I can't wait for it to be daylight.

Ma goes to work the next day and my cousin and I examine the bike before taking it out on the sidewalk.

"Get on!" he commands.

I sit on the bike and he stands on the back, leaning over me to grab on to the handles, and we push off. In seconds we are flying down the sidewalk, going so fast my feet can't stay on the pedals. I can hear him giggling in my ear but he is going too fast for me.

"Stop!" I scream.

But he can't because it is too exciting and wonderful to stop, and he keeps on going until we fall over. My cousin laughs, but I have a cut on my knee and begin to cry.

"Are you okay?" He is about to help me up when we hear, "¡Sinvergüenza! ¡Hijo de puta!" It is his mother, Bon Bon, coming upon us. Thwack! She beats him about the head and back into the house screaming insults. Zoraida, Eddie's half sister, tries to distract Bon Bon.

"Mami . . ."

But she can't be distracted, and Bon Bon beats Little Eddie until she is spent.

Then there is sorry quiet as Zoraida takes her brother into the bathroom and calms him with cool running water. When they come out his white skin is clean and polished, his hair cleanly parted on the side, combed over into a pompadour. The only evidence of what had just happened is a Band-Aid over his eye. Zoraida soothes him with a toy plane, then watches carefully as Little Eddie approaches his disoriented mother.

"Mami, look," he says sweetly, flying the plane in front of her eyes. "Look at the little plane, look how it flies." Bon Bon's eyes are too glazed over to notice.

"Look, Mami . . ."

Her wild eyes finally focus and she smiles weakly at her son. I am numb and though my crying started the whole thing it is like I am not there.

The next day Zoraida is making us breakfast. The eggs she fries are sizzling on the hot stove.

"My mother puts my hands on the stove," she says matter-of-factly.

"Why?" I ask her.

"To teach me not to steal."

I listen to the sizzling eggs. They crackle done and she serves us.

"It's the only way to teach children," Zoraida insists.

I eat my eggs but wonder if it was hands on a hot surface or hands in the flames that taught the lesson.

Evenings after Ma comes from work we sit on the porch and look down the walkway into the street. Warning us kids, Bon Bon places a voodoo coconut head at the end of the path.

"Don't go past that head. If you do it will bite at your legs."

Ma pulls me to her and sighs with weariness and I see that her bruises have gone from black to yellow. Inside the house, Bon Bon has had a personality transformation. She is now kindly and tenderly tending her husband's, my uncle's, aching feet with baby powder. The transformation lasts into the next morning and she is cheerful.

"Do you like Gina Lollobrigida's hair?" she asks me.

"Who?"

"Gina Lollobrigida, that Italian movie star with the boy cut."

I don't know who she is talking about, but I go along with whatever she wants. Zoraida glances at me, and Bon Bon smiles like the three of us are girlfriends. I can play that game but I wonder where Little Eddie and his toy plane are.

Bon Bon puts newspapers under a kitchen chair and calls Zoraida and me into the room to play beauty parlor except Bon Bon is the only one with the scissors. Zoraida goes first. Snip! One long lock of hair drifts to the floor. Snip! Another one. It doesn't stop until Zoraida looks like Joan of Arc. We both smile hard and no one speaks. Then it's my turn. I'm sitting in the chair and it's so quiet I can hear the scissors struggle and saw through my thick, wavy mane. Afraid one of my ears will hit the ground along with a curl or two, I sit perfectly still. When she is done Bon Bon beams with satisfaction and gazes at me like *I* look at my dolls. I find my reflection somewhere. My hair is cut to the middle of my ear and it doesn't curl pretty anymore—it is dry and frizzy and I look like a piece of broccoli and wonder if that's the style.

As the sky darkens and my mother is due home from work, Bon Bon gets excited.

"We will surprise your mother," she tells me.

"Come quick, Zoraida," she commands her daughter.

Zoraida goes along like we are getting off easy. Bon Bon makes us hold each other's hands across our bodies like ballet dancers.

"*Así*," she instructs, positioning us like we are her dolls.

Then she takes a peek out of the window. Suddenly—"Here she comes! Quick—turn your heads and look at the corner."

Zoraida and I stare at each other.

"Like this!" She adjusts us once again, turning our heads to look at a wall at the exact same angle.

My mother comes in exhausted, and it is only when I see her jaw practically hit the ground in despair that I realize how I must look.

The next day we go home, where my father pleads, tears running down his face.

"Please forgive me. I didn't know what I was doing. I lost my mind. It was the rum."

My mother rises on her toes, pointing to the radiator and the fading bruises on her arms and face. "Look at me! *¡Abusador! ¡Animal! ¡Loco! ¡Sinvergüenza!*"

"I don't remember anything! Please forgive me. Just stay and I'll sleep in a corner. Please . . . ! Forgive me. I don't know what I was doing. I was drunk. I went crazy. I promise it won't ever happen again. It wasn't my fault. It was the rum. I love you. I can't live without you."

Then he crumples down in a heap beside the flowered sofa and weeps. I look to my mother but I am stuck because I don't know what I want to happen, and a lump forms in my throat that threatens to choke me as my heart breaks for him.

I stand, watching him weak and falling apart, and Ma strong and vengeful. I don't know whose side I am on.

CHAPTER 3

Poverty Sing-Along

S itting at my mother's swollen ankles, I am fascinated by poking them and timing how long the indention takes to fill out.

"*Muchacha*," she says before shooing me away. It's Friday and the whole family, including Uncle Frank; his wife, Iris; and the cousins are shopping for the week at Don Joe's. Iris has begun to wear high heels all the time; Mickey's snot has not moved since I first saw him.

"His snot looks like candle wax," Ma had said and the idea stays with me. But now in the soft light coming from the greasy bulb hanging from the ceiling I notice how her foot makes a right angle as she calls out her order.

"*Una libra de cebollas.*"

Friendly Don Joe gathers the onions for her, not his brother and co-owner Don Tito, whose smiles are so fleeting they look like tics.

It's clear to me that riding that ankle would be as great as a ride on *la macchina*, the merry-go-round on the back of a pickup truck, driven up Third Avenue by an Italian guy who charges twenty-five cents for a ride. Don Joe weighs the brown paper bag of onions, puts it in a box, and writes what Ma will owe him in his black-and-white composition notebook. The neighborhood owes him so much money and he's turned the pages so many times there is a bump of paper where he clutches to turn the pages.

I try sitting on her foot, but she lets her foot go slack and I am sent tumbling onto the soft sawdust-covered floor.

"Go play with your cousins," she exclaims.

Chaty and Mickey have found a book of matches and are experimenting with them, and Mimi is lounging around looking bored, and I'm glad they are here so it won't be a bruised-mother-broken-furniture Friday, but I am not interested in playing with them. I'm more interested in my mother's leg and foot. Doña Cabeza comes in and buys some coffee and I am once again surprised that such movie-star-red hair surrounds such a wrinkly, ugly face. Mean Genoveva buys cotton and alcohol to apply her shots of penicillin to neighborhood children, and picks her nose on her way out. Flor comes in and all the men admire her big behind and she smiles, revealing missing front teeth. La Puerca/Bizca walks in past Ma and my aunt Iris, who try not to laugh when they see dirt outlines of her breasts on the back of her dress.

"Wearing the dirty part to the back doesn't fool me. I still know she hasn't washed that dress in ages," snickers Ma. Her pregnant-lady blouse hits the top of the wooden crate she sits on. I make two dents in my mother's swollen leg and watch it poke back out before I make another one.

"¿Qué más, doña Isa?" asks Don Joe.

"Cinco libras de arroz," says Ma. Don Joe scoops out some rice, pours it into a brown paper bag, folds the top over, then karate chops it at just the right angle and just hard enough to seal it, and laughs.

"The factory has so much work," Iris says to Ma. "I can work twelve hours a day if I want to. Fabulous."

"There's always a lot of piecework," says Ma.

"I'm happy with it."

"It's okay, but I like to put the whole dress together. *Más interesante.*"

"Well, you speak English better . . ."

"As soon as I got off that plane from Puerto Rico—my brother Eddie helped me learn how to say 'thread' and 'needle' and everything else I have to say in English. It was hard but I did it!"

"Did you come on those tiny World War Two planes, too?" asks Don Joe.

"*Sí, sí. AveMaríaPurísima,* what a trip; we sat along the sides of the plane like soldiers do before jumping out. All we could afford." Then she starts laughing. "It's funny now, but not then. No. No. Did I tell you, Iris, about the poor barber traveling with us?"

"*Sí, sí,* but tell it again."

"*El pobre* had all his tools in a cardboard box. Scissors, clippers, brushes, razors, but every time the plane angled in one *dirección* or another . . ."

She's laughing so hard she can barely go on.

". . . the box with all the tools went spilling out, *traka, traka, traka* across the plane to the other side. And he . . . he . . ."

Don Joe brings her a glass of water. She gulps it down. "*Gracias, Don Joe,*" and then she continues. "As soon as he picks his barber tools up and goes to the other side and sits, the plane angles in the other direction and out, *traka, traka, traka* go his scissors, clippers, brushes all over again. It got to the point everybody was just waiting to catch a comb or a brush for him for our entertainment."

I see my chance to try to make a dent in her ankle again.

"Stop, *mija*," she says, shaking her foot.

Then she turns her attention back to her shopping. "Five pounds of beans *y nada más*."

Don Joe gives the same karate treatment to five pounds of beans. Chewing on the end of a red carpenter's pencil to sharpen it, he adds the new debt to our old debt, and Iris begins *her* shopping.

Finally the shopping is done. Iris calls Uncle Frank, who has been drinking outside with my father. They leave the milk crates they had been precariously sitting on, come in, throw their boxes of food onto their shoulders, and he-man it out of the store.

Uncle Frank yells to Chaty to leave the matches alone. Chaty ignores him and slips them into his pocket. We all step over Moncho, the bum who sleeps in the building's doorway. Entering, we hear metal hitting each step above us. It's Americanized Lydia pulling her son, Dennis, up the stairs, his polio braces making the noise. Dennis is always either sleeping out on the street or dancing the mambo, braces and all. We step around them.

"*Drogas*, Dennis is a drug addict," says Pops the minute we get into our apartment.

Chaty and Mickey and I jump back and forth from the sofa to the chair, careful our feet don't touch the ground because we have decided the floor is quicksand.

"What's quicksand?" asks Mickey.

Something is wrong with Mickey's brain so Chaty helps him understand what we are playing. "Never mind—it's fire, Mickey, make believe it's fire."

"Stop jumping around," screams Mimi, rubbing her head. "I'm trying to watch television."

She always looks so sweaty and hot. Chaty uses matches to help Mickey explore under the bed and I stay near the kitchen to listen. Ma makes coffee for all as Iris peels the plantains.

"Did you hear the one about the *jíbaro* who was so stupid he tried to blow out the electric light with his hat?" says my uncle Frank and they all laugh.

"What about the sugarcane worker who kept infecting his wound so that the government would keep giving him money?" says Pops, making them all laugh even harder. I wonder why they laugh—it's not funny.

"*La pobreza.* When my mother died we were really starving with no one to take care of us—remember, Franco?"

"*Sí,* I remember that but I don't remember our mother."

"If I was five years old when she died you must've been three," says Ma.

Then they turn to my father like he's done something wrong.

"When was the last time you visited your mother?" asks Uncle Eddie.

My father says nothing.

"If my mother was alive," says Franco, "I would carry her on my back."

My father grunts and leaves the room as I picture my tall, skinny grandmother being carried by my father, piggyback style. Iris changes the subject.

"You knew which kids had worms because they had big stomachs."

"Thank God, they tore down that horrible slum El Fanguito."

My father returns with his guitar. The horribleness of Puerto Rico makes everyone want to sing about it. The song, about a poor country hick who works like a slave only to be horribly disappointed when he can't sell his goods in town, is a beautiful song that stabs me in my heart like a knife that stays there. I hear more and more happy/sad songs until it's time for my uncle and his family to leave or I fall asleep on the sofa.

The baby inside Ma grows until she gets tired and lazy and wants me to run errands for her. I love it when she sends me to the store all by myself.

"Can you do it?" Ma asks. "Can you get *un aguacate para hoy*? Just go and ask Don Joe for an avocado for today and come right back. Don't talk to anyone but Don Joe."

I got it. I can do this, I think. An avocado for today—not for tomorrow or the day after, but for today! *"Un aguacate para hoy,"* I repeat. I figure out how I will remember—I will repeat it over and over in my head until I get to the store, and then say it out loud as soon as I enter and see Don Joe. Perfect. Flying down the stairs repeating, *"Un aguacate para hoy, un aguacate para hoy, un aguacate para hoy..."* I enter—but it's not Don Joe—it's Don Tito, and everything flies out of my mind.

"Hola, Sonia, ¿qué tal?" He gives me his lightning-quick tic smile.

I stare at him—what was it? What was it I wanted?

"¿Que necesitas, hija?"

My mind is a total blank. I run outside and scream up to the window until Ma sticks her head out.

"Ma, I forgot."

Her eyes roll before she goes in and then tosses down a piece of paper weighed down with some coins. Catching it, I solemnly go back into the store. Don Tito reads the note, feels up the avocados, and shakes them near his ear until he picks the perfect one to be eaten today.

"Here," he says. "Must be eaten today—not tomorrow—today."

After he writes up our purchase in his notebook, he hands me the avocado in a bag and goes back to chopping up some pork.

What a dope I am, not being able to remember anything, I think, as I see a tray of coconut candy covered over with wax paper. Watching the flies trying to sneak in under the wax paper and onto the candy I remember a household conversation, "No money, no money, no money, we got no money," and I get a great idea. Don Tito has forgotten I am there—so I steal the candy and run upstairs.

Ma is happy about the *aguacate* and having her all to myself makes me want to share my stolen candy with her.

"Hmmm," she says, rubbing her belly, "so *delicioso*—but don't buy anything on credit again unless you tell me, okay?"

"But I didn't buy it, Ma," I say, chewing. "It's free."

"Don Joe gave it to you?"

"Don Joe wasn't there—it was Don Tito."

"He gave it to you?"

"Nobody gave it to me. I stole it."

Ma stops chewing.

"You what?"

"I stole it. I got it for free."

She swallows and looks at me very seriously.

"It is very bad to steal. You must never steal."

"But you always say we don't have any money . . ."

"No, no, no. Never mind that. When you steal it breaks the Virgin Mary's heart and she cries."

"How do you know that?"

"I know because it rains."

"What?"

"Yes, when it rains it is the Virgin Mary crying because children have done something bad. You must go downstairs—here—give Don Tito these three pennies and tell him that you are sorry."

I go downstairs.

"*Hola*, Sonia, can I help you?"

"*Sí* . . ." But I don't say anything. I am too scared. He looks at me, waiting.

"Is the *aguacate* okay . . . ?"

"I . . . er . . . I . . ." I try to get brave enough to tell him I'm sorry but I can't.

Don Tito sighs and because he is used to the whole neighborhood hanging out in his store he finally goes to the back, saying, "When you think of what you want, let me know, okay?"

I look at all the flies stuck to the tape hanging from the ceiling and then count all the cans of tomato sauce on the shelves. Finally I figure out what to do. Since I'm doing this because of the Virgin Mary, I kiss the three pennies up to heaven where she hangs out, leave them on the counter, and run out!

"Sonia . . . !" he calls out as I reach the door but I don't turn back. I just keep going and running up the stairs, thinking about the Virgin Mary crying every time some kid did something bad in the Bronx.

Then, in the middle of one night soon after, I hear Ma scurrying around her room putting a nightgown into a small valise and I see Pops pulling on his pants. When I go to their room to investigate I'm shushed back into bed. I don't know where she's gone but it has something to do with the baby. In the days I wait for her to return I stay close to my father. One day he decides to work on his car across the street from our building and I watch him open the hood and look around and wrestle with something deep inside. Finally he pulls himself out, opens the trunk, and hands me a jar.

"Go to Don Joe's and get me some water."

I'm glad to be sent on an errand like Ma sent me. He waits until the Third Avenue traffic is clear.

"Go now," he commands.

I run across the street and get the water, but on my way back I watch a coal delivery. The coal skips and tumbles down a chute, feeding our hungry building. I don't know how long I watch before I realize that I've been watching too long, and I suddenly bolt across the street when a black car comes just close enough to twirl me. I manage to keep the water from spilling. The car slows down as I shoot a look across the street to see if my father had seen. When the man in the car sees I am still standing he speeds off as I sigh, relieved my father is still working under the hood, his ass sticking out.

I'm glad he didn't see because he would've scolded about how I never pay attention and how I deserve that the "lap" will be taken away from me when the new baby comes anyway. *Who cares?* I think. Can a new baby run across the street, almost get hit by a car, and not spill a drop of water?

Ma comes home from the hospital with Joe and a great fuss is made and all the grown-ups tease me even more about how my mother's "lap" has been taken away from me. I know what they mean—they mean that now Joe will be the baby of the house.

Weeks later Joe is sick and the room the crib is in is spooky and gloomy with candles. He lies there naked, looking tiny and lost, as mean Genoveva gives out medical advice and my worried mother hovers over him. I am just tall enough to see into his crib and his smallness panics me. I want someone to pick him up and wrap him in a blanket, and take care of him because he is a boy and special, not an old *chancleta*, an old slipper like me. I know boys are better than girls because neighbor women always groan with disappointment when they hear anybody's had a girl. They even curse the mother's bad luck. So I wonder why they don't just pick Joe up instead of standing around—but I can't get them to look down at me for my opinion, so I wander around the apartment until I fall asleep on the sofa.

The next day I watch cartoons. There is one with submarines and bombs going off and funny bad guys with little square mustaches right under their noses who hold their right arms straight out to say "hello." In an ocean scene a tube with a big eye comes out of the water and chases the submarine all over the place. In between the cartoons are commercials for chocolate candy. The delicious melted chocolate is poured from one container to another in slow, tempting ways and I get really hungry. I go into Joe's sickroom.

"Ma . . ."

"What?"

Then she suddenly knows what I want and we go into the kitchen where she gives me a bowl of canned fruit that had been in the refrigerator for a few days and goes back to Joe. I sit at the table and start to eat when I see a small black thing in it. I look closely and I think it's a tiny roach.

"Ma, look!"

She comes running in, looking all scattered and busy.

"What is it?"

"There is something in my fruit."

She looks quickly but sees nothing.

"Where? Where?"

"There"—I point—"don't you see . . . ?"

But then Joe makes a tiny wail.

"It's fine, just eat it . . ."

She runs back to him. I look in my food again. This time I am absolutely sure there is a roach in it. So I eat around it, but my stomach feels jumpy and I don't understand why—I usually love Del Monte fruit cocktail.

That night I sleep in my bed and not the sofa and a scraping metal sound wakes me up. I am facing away from the wall but I know that it is the big eye from the submarine in the cartoon come to visit. I can feel it watching and screeching along with my every move. When I breathe it leans in so close I can feel its breath on the back of my neck. I am paralyzed with fear and too scared to move even though I can hear Aurea and Ma in the kitchen and really have to pee. If I scream or yell, the eye will get me.

Finally Ma comes in carrying Joe.

"*¿Qué te pasa?*"

I try to signal her with my eyes but she doesn't react—can't she see the eye thing behind me?

"Come and eat . . ."

I get up, balancing a puddle of fear in the small of my back.

"Hurry up," she says.

And when I turn and look behind me, the eye is gone!

"What's the matter with you?" says Ma. By this time Aurea has joined us. I tell them about the eye. They listen to my every word like it was the most important word they will ever hear, or like there is a worm coming out of my nose. They are both fascinated and horrified.

"You dreamed it," says Aurea.

"Of course you did," adds my mother, eyeing me suspiciously and feeling my head for a fever. "Don't you dare get sick!"

"No, it was here," I insist.

"Don't be stupid," says Aurea. "There was no periscope. You dreamed it. Come on, let's eat." Then they both turn away.

"Wait," I add. They turn back and wait.

"Not only that, Ma beat me with a wire clothes hanger yesterday."

"What?" my mother screeches.

"You did, you did!" I insist.

"Where do you get such nutty ideas? I've never done that in my life and I would never do that! Are you crazy?"

I believe what I say though I know it never happened.

When Joe is stronger and it gets warmer we go to the beach with Grandmother but nobody likes it. Grandmother hates the harsh wind. Pops hates the sand getting into his black shoes and socks. Ma hates that her heels dig into the sand, and Joe is just a baby; and whose idea was it to come to the beach anyway? I look at all the happy families hiding under bright umbrellas, dressed in shorts and sandals while the grown-ups in my group are in Sunday clothes. Aurea is allowed to play at the shore. I am happy digging in the sand, looking busy so I can watch her, a dark stick figure in the brightness, and listen to the grown-ups.

"What happened to your woman Juana?" asks Grandmother.

"*Na*, nothing, she was just . . . nobody . . . really . . ."

"You were with her a couple of years," says Ma, bored.

"Kid stuff. She never loved me," says Pops.

I stop digging—I just know that Ma couldn't have had another husband—only bad women have many husbands—but if Pops had a wife, maybe Aurea was his kid, right? No—they hate each other. I go back to digging and getting nowhere.

Grandmother compares Rockaway Beach to beaches in Puerto Rico. I look out and wonder if that bit of land I see beyond the waves of Rockaway Beach *is* Puerto Rico. She complains about the cold.

"*¡Esta playa está muy fría!*" says Grandmother.

Everyone mumbles in agreement. "Yes, it is cold at this beach . . ." And then there is silence.

"*¿Una silla?*" My father offers his mother a beach chair.

She grabs it from him and tries to open it herself. Her hands are like claws. When engrossed in a task she mutters "*Perate, perate, perate,*" meaning wait, under her breath until she sounds motorized. "Wait, wait, wait" for what?

"*Perate, perate, perate . . .*" she says while she tries to figure out how the chair works. Suddenly she curses "*¡Mal rayo te parta!*" as in her final efforts to open the chair she breaks a finger. My father bows his head like it was his fault and she ignores him.

We have to pack up our blankets and sandwiches and beer and take her to a hospital emergency room.

Later on at home as Ma undresses I roam around the room, and looking for something to play with in the drawers I come across a picture of Aurea as a girl about my size. She looks so cute but is standing on a wooden sidewalk in front of a broken-down wooden house. Was this place El Fanguito, where babies drown underneath the houses? Then suddenly I know something! Or maybe I always knew it but it just came up. Or maybe I knew and forgot. However it happened I know this—Aurea has a different father from me! And I

33

even remember hearing his name! It was Aureo! Aureo Andino! It's just like her name except with an "o" at the end! Yes, yes, how could I have forgotten an old story I had heard in the kitchen or in the sound waves that floated around the apartment—Ma had said she and Aurea had been downtown once and seen a man Ma had pointed to and said, "That's your father, Aurea Andino."

Ma has her leg up on the bed and is slipping off the stocking she wore to the beach when I understand this.

"Ma, you are Aurea's mother but she has a different father named Aureo, right? Aureo Andino, right, right?" My mind loves it when something is clear! But Ma stops stripping her stocking off midcalf and shoots me such a hard look I feel stabbed in the head.

"Don't you ever mention that name is this house again." And her stabbing look holds my emotions dangling in the air until I know she means business. But who cares—I know I have a sister!

CHAPTER 4

Invisible Girl

I am invisible or at least fading away.

Genoveva takes me to school and we are almost out the door when I remember—"My tissue! I need a tissue!" I am so happy I remembered this time.

"AveMaríaPurísima," exclaims Ma, running into the bathroom and tearing off a piece of toilet paper. "Here—a tissue, okay?" I stand there in hat, scarf, gloves, and coat and she becomes irritated that she'll have to undress me in order to shove the tissue into my skirt pocket. *"Paciencia,"* she says, stretching her fingers up to the heavens in despair. Pulling and shoving and unbuttoning and jamming the tissue into my pocket she kisses me bluntly and, like I'm dust on a broom, shakes me out the door.

P.S. 4 is old and beautiful with tall windows that must be opened with mean-looking hooks on the ends of long poles, and fancy fan-shaped windows over doors way above my head. I'm in kindergarten and all we do is play. I can't wait to set up the blocks to play my favorite game—jumping out a window of a burning apartment! I practice so I'm not like those kids in the newspaper who always die because they are afraid to jump.

"Coats off, everybody," sings my pretty teacher. First I take off my gloves, then my hat, then my scarf, then my coat, then my sweater, then my blouse, then my skirt, and suddenly I realize I'm down to my slip! Ma had dressed me in so many clothes I got on a roll and couldn't stop undressing. This strikes me as funny but when I look around I see no one has noticed. How can that be?

I put my clothes back on and play jumping out the window but the boy all set to catch me walks away and I lie sprawled on the rug. Did he not see me flying toward him? Later as we sit around in a circle, the pretty teacher asks each of us to show her our handkerchiefs or tissues. I am proud when she gets to me because for once I haven't forgotten.

"Where is your handkerchief or tissue, Sonia?"

I show her proudly. She grabs it from my hand and lets it unfold in neat little squares so that everyone can see, then asks me, "Is this a tissue? Is it?"

I see a tissue; doesn't she see a tissue?

"Look, everybody, this is what Sonia's family thinks is a tissue."

But it *is* a tissue. Why can't she see that?

"I sure don't see a tissue," she says, reaching into her handbag and pulling out a Kleenex. "This is a tissue."

I still don't see the difference.

At home Ma does not see that I cannot keep my panties up. They are so old and the elastic is so stretched they dance loosely around my hips. I take two steps and they slip down to my thighs, two more and they are around my ankles—the only solution is to hold them up through my dress. So for days I clutch them in my fist as I go to school and it almost works until older boys surround me at recess and stick their fingers up my leg. I kick and kick and kick as hard as possible, but can only hit them with one hand because the other one is holding up my panties. The only thing that makes them stop is when they hear the recess bell that signals that playtime is over. They run away from me but I can still feel their fingers.

I am late returning with my bedraggled dress and my white collar all torn. "Why are you late?" asks Mr. Applebaum, the principal, when he sees me. I tell him what happened.

"That's what you get for playing with boys," he says, his face looming at me, his big, fleshy nose practically touching my own. "And let go of your dress!" I switch hands, holding up my panties as I go back to my classroom.

At home I wait for Ma to see if she notices me.

"Let me just have my coffee, please," she begs coming in. I watch her fix herself some syrupy strong *café* and sink into her seat. After a moment she puts her head in her hands and sits quietly but even then it looks like she is struggling. When she doesn't rise or even drink her coffee I move away. Wandering around the apartment I notice that my ankles are encrusted with dirt and it surprises me. I had only seen dirt embedded in skin on Moncho the bum's cheekbones, or on the ankles of the Gypsy children who came through our neighborhood and lived in storefronts. How long had my ankles been like that? Had I been invisible to myself? Remarkable! Incredible! The dirt moves as I flex and point my foot, and I feel I must show someone this fantastic phenomenon so I go into my sister's room. Standing by her door, I check out her mood, wait for her to turn around and talk to me, but she shoots me a baleful glare instead. She's working on a movie-star photo album, pictures of Tony Curtis and Janet Leigh, the most beautiful actors of all time. She concentrates, gluing a heart by each of their faces and connecting those hearts with a skinny pink ribbon. I slither closer and sit on her bed to watch but she ignores me so I creep over to a jar of pencils.

"Don't touch that!"

So I go over to her stack of construction paper.

"Get away."

I wish she would let me touch her paper and pencils, but she turns back to her project furiously. The album is so big you can sit on it like a stool. But I have something to show, too.

"Want to see something . . . ?" I tease.

"No."

"Look." I show her my ankles.

"That's disgusting! Maaaaaa!"

Ma comes in. "What?"

"Look!"

Ma looks at my ankles, then marches me into the bathroom, where she sees a roach in the tub.

Just last week Ma had set off a roach bomb. When it was safe to come back home every surface was covered with roach carcasses, their feet comically sticking up into the air. Triumphantly sweeping them into a pile in the middle of the room the way people on television piled up leaves in the middle of their lawns in the fall, Ma's eyes had shone with the joy of success and conquest. Wetting one edge of a newspaper, sticking it on the floor to be used as a dustpan, and sweeping all the papery roach bodies onto the paper she cracked, "We don't got a lot but we sure got a lot of roaches."

So the one roach in the tub that had escaped death really pisses her off. After squashing the roach and swishing it down the drain, she makes me get into the tub.

I get in and wait for the warm water to rise up above my caked ankles. "And don't forget to clean your knees and elbows, too," she adds, flying out the door yelling for my sister.

"Aurea, help me defrost the refrigerator!"

I scrub my ankles until they are sparkling clean. But when I start to scrub my knees the movement of the washcloth reminds me of the hem of a skirt, so I drape the edge of the washcloth over my knee and make believe it's my hemline. Then I drape it over my shoulder and make a fancy sleeve; across my crotch it makes a bathing suit bottom . . .

"What are you doing?" Ma is back!

I stare at her from my watery fashion world.

"I tol' you to scrub your ankles! Look—if you don't scrub your knees and ankles and elbows they will turn to tin! Do it!" Punctuating her statement with a slam of the door she leaves again. I think about what she said in the wake of her exasperation. Had she said "tin"? That my knees would turn into tin? Like the tin in the Tin Man in *The Wizard of Oz*? Bent they looked pretty good but straightened they looked pretty dark. Was that dirt? I scrub then reexamine them, but they don't look any cleaner no matter how much I scrub. Then they start to feel a little stiff. Oh no, I can't bend them. Oh my God! Oh my God! I'll never walk again! I feel my face get hard as tin as well with the only movement being snot and tears running down to my chin. Ma bursts back into the room.

"*¿Qué te pasa?*"

"My knees have turned to tin."

She stares. After a moment she sinks to the floor, leans against the wall, and puts her hands on her knees; then, placing her head on her arms, she rests. I stop crying to look at her.

"What's the matter?"

She doesn't say a word and it is silent and serious.

"Ma . . . ?"

But she doesn't hear me as she finally crawls over to me, wipes my face with the washcloth, helps me out of the tub, dries me off, and gets me into pajamas. As we march through the living room, I see warm light slipping out from underneath the door of my sister's room and in bed I dream about pencils and paper.

School has plenty of pencils and paper and even crayons. When it's Halloween we draw pumpkins and leaf shapes and cut them out with safe scissors. "Color them all the beautiful colors of the fall," says the teacher. "Yellow, and orange, and gold, and purple."

I think she is silly for telling me that leaves come in yellow and orange and gold and purple because everybody knows leaves come in green then turn brown before dropping dead to the ground. But I do what she says so I can use all the crayons. I'll even make blue leaves if it'll make her happy.

"Very nice, Sonia. We'll put your leaves on the windows."

On the block Aurea and I dress up as hoboes to go trick-or-treating. We run in and out and up and down the buildings, knocking on every door, and people give us money! And it's fun and wonderful but we look over our shoulders for the crazy white boys from other neighborhoods who don't know enough to dress up like anything at all and come armed with long stockings full of colored chalk. Suddenly they are upon us.

"Here they come! Run!" says Aurea.

Thwack! A boy with spiky yellow hair and green teeth hits her with his sock before hitting me, leaving a cloudy streak of pink down both our backs. It doesn't hurt but we scream and shriek and try to get away, but not really. By the time we straggle back home we look like hoboes dressed up as rainbows.

"What happened to you two?" says Ma. *"Maronna!"*

Ma is working with Italian seamstresses and likes to sound like them.

The next day at school the teacher asks what we did for Halloween. I tell her we dressed up as hoboes and got money . . .

"Money? Not candy or treats . . . ?"

"No . . ." I say carefully.

"What did you do with the money?"

What a stupid question, I think, but I answer, "Bought candy."

She is so shocked she sputters. "If you are going to get money . . . you should at least give it to UNICEF . . ."

Give our money away? She must be crazy, so I don't even bother telling her about the white boys beating us with colored socks. She'd never get it.

CHAPTER 5

A Christmas Fact of Life

S hould we tell her?" Mimi asks her brother Chaty. She is pale and thin with a bright, sweaty, sick look, as always.

"No, don't," he answers.

I am not sure I want to know what they don't want to tell me. We are in their living room waiting for Iris to come home. The television's horizontal hold has been broken for about a year but the constant scroll does not seem to bother anyone, least of all Mickey, who is sitting two feet from the screen, his pointy face mesmerized by what he is seeing. I guess, with his brain trouble, it looks fine to him.

"Let's tell her," Mimi says.

"Tell me," I say.

"No," says Chaty.

"But she wants to know," says Mimi.

They go back and forth a few times but then Mimi asks, "How do we get presents for Christmas?"

"Santa Claus . . ." I say cautiously. I don't know if I should tell them the whole story. How Santa magically dissolves the window behind our Christmas tree, carefully creeps around it, leaves our presents, and then creeps out and magically puts the window back.

"Why does he leave some presents for us at *your* house?" she challenges.

Saves time, I think. If Santa had to wait for us Puerto Ricans to stop partying on Christmas Eve and go to bed, he'd never finish delivering gifts and we would hold up the whole world getting presents. That's why Santa often drops off presents for the whole family at one relative's house. But I don't say that—the looks and grins going on between Mimi and Chaty make me suspicious.

"Come look," she says finally. We go into the boys' room. It's so small the door hits the bunk bed against the wall. Both beds are a tangled mess of clothes and sheets shiny with gray dirt. The window faces the courtyard but there is some sooty light coming in through it. Mimi opens the door to a small closet. "Look," she says. At the top of the closet are boxes wrapped in bright red-and-green paper and pretty golden bows.

"Those are the presents for Christmas. Our parents bought them. There is no Santa Claus," she says.

I back out of the room slowly, not knowing where to put this news. My back? My lap? The floor. We sit and watch the television scrolling endlessly for a while because no one knows what to say. Chaty finally provokes Mickey until Mickey wrestles Chaty to the ground to fart on his head. When it's time for me to go, Mimi suddenly blurts out, "Okay, look—there *is* a Santa Claus. We were just kidding . . ."

"Yeah, right . . ." adds Chaty.

I don't answer and just take my new burden with me. When I get home my parents are fighting over a suckling pig on the table. It's pink with some spiky black hairs.

"What am I supposed to do with this?" Ma barks.

"What do you think, prepare it!" Pops laughs, walking out the door.

"I hate this shit . . ." she exclaims once he is gone.

I think about Santa—that traitor.

"Go get Genoveva," she tells me.

I do. She comes up. *"¿Qué pasó?"*

"Look at this," says Ma, sniffling like she doesn't know what it is. "I've never prepared a thing like this."

I don't understand what's going on. First the news about Santa Claus and now my mother forgets how to cook?

"You just grind up some garlic, and oregano, and olive oil, and vinegar, and slap it on the pig," says Genoveva.

"Really?" says Ma, looking helpless, as if she's never heard of those ingredients before in her life.

"Look, I'll show you," says Genoveva. And she gets the wooden pestle and grinds some garlic, adds the other stuff, and makes a paste. "See?" she says when she's done.

"Now what?" says Ma weakly.

"Well, you make holes in the pig and stuff it with this stuff."

My mother looks like she's forgotten how to understand both English and Spanish. Genoveva picks up a knife and starts to stab the pink suckling pig all over. It looks like she is stabbing a baby, then sticking vinegar and garlic in the wounds, so I leave and look at our Christmas tree to ponder Santa Claus and make up stories about the ornaments like I always do. The horse ornament is on its way to meet the mouse ornament to take it for a ride, and they will stop to eat a little bit of candy cane, then pick up the angel, who will ride on the mouse's head to the top of the tree. It doesn't matter about Santa Claus.

I hear the door. It's my father.

"*Now* what do I do with this pig?" says Ma. "I told you it won't fit in the oven!"

"Why are you worried? I'm going to take it to Valencia Bakery. They will roast it for me."

I go into the kitchen in time to see him stuffing the pig into a cardboard box to take it to the bakery. Hours later he comes back with the cooked pig on his back.

"Wonderful," says Ma, snitching off a little piece of crackling.

"I guess you haven't forgotten how to eat it," my father teases.

I go to the window to wait for the Christmas Eve eruption. It is snowing and I'm hoping it stops. Even though there are a thousand, million songs about how swell a white Christmas is, and every picture of Christmas you draw in school has to have snow, we always pray for it *not* to snow because after we celebrate here, we will get into our cars and drive to someone else's house to party.

Instantaneously the apartment is full of relatives and all the neighbors in the building. Flor wearing a tight skirt and stockings with a seam up the back, Iris wearing high heels, the cousins from Fulton Avenue, and Little Eddie—who pulls me aside.

"Let's stay awake all night and catch Santa."

I look at him and wonder if he's kidding, if he knows that there is no Santa, too. Kitchen chairs are brought into the living room. Uncle Eddie tunes his guitar, somebody scrapes on a *güiro* with a fork, and Ma sings an *aguinaldo*. Uncle Frank is so delighted with his siblings that he claps, not like an adult but like a kid playing pattycake, sitting in a chair with his feet slightly running in place. My father doesn't know where to look he is so cheerful, and I feel that Ma is better than the other mothers who cook and serve because my mother can sing.

Their song ends. "Bravo . . ." Everybody claps. Then there is a commotion of chairs scraping and guitar tuning, toasts and shots of rum being drunk. No matter how hard I watch I never see Ma and Uncle Eddie signal each other to start the next song; I never even notice them deciding which song to sing next.

They take a break for food and drink. Eddie and I and the Fulton cousins whirl around. The Fulton cousins have forgotten what they've told me. Chaty takes off and the rest follow; we fly around faster and faster, and then we try to knock each other over, or trip each other as we wait, wildly, for anything to happen.

Chano the singer appears at our door. I only see him once a year when he follows my uncle around to sing *aguinaldos* and he always looks the same. A small man in a pale blue suit, thin socks, and pointy black shoes, his hair is unbelievably thick and wavy; his face looks like it was carved out of a rock and his eyes are slanted up.

Like a movie star he steps around the police lock, throws his head back, and starts to sing a made-up lyric about what my mother is wearing and how generous my father is with the *coquito*, a creamy coconut drink I'm not allowed to have because it has rum. Each lyric is more clever and funnier than the previous one. But then he sings of the birth of Jesus.

"Ya vendrán los reyes . . ."

And it is still the most beautiful story I ever heard, whether there is a Santa Claus or not.

By this time the small flame of a party has erupted into a three-alarm blaze and several songs later it is time to move on. We are on fire with love and music and sadness for the poor little baby in the manger.

Little Eddie and I and the cousins travel down the stairs and out onto the street, riding the wave of mothers juggling food and little kids, their high heels slipping into the snow, and men holding guitars over their heads. We pile into our jalopies, and with tires spinning in the snow we take off to someone else's block. There, we do the same thing—making the *parranda* a longer and longer parade of revelers as we travel, slipping and sliding all over the Bronx.

And then it's Christmas morning. And I wake up with my face stuck on Iris's plastic-covered sofa and Little Eddie is holding his face in his hands, staring at me like an owl.

"We didn't make it," he says as I unstick myself from the sofa.

"No . . ."

"We fell asleep and missed Santa . . ."

"Merry Christmas, Sonia," says Iris, handing me a tea set exactly like the tea set she handed me last year.

Christmas Day is spent in a daze of exhaustion, and it's bedtime before I tell Ma what I know about Santa Claus.

"Who told you?" she says, annoyed.

"Mimi and Chaty."

She grits her teeth. "Stupid asses."

But it's really okay with me. I drift off to sleep comforted that the story about baby Jesus is just as unbelievable as Santa Claus and no one says that *that* story's not true.

"¡Guerra! ¡Guerra interplanetaria!"

I'm awakened by Pops screeching and I shoot straight up out of a deep sleep. What? What! My heart beats a hundred times per minute. But I'm confused. It's morning, daytime—bad things only happen at night. My father comes into my room.

"¡Cállate!"

We lock eyes as he tells me to shut up. I stare back and realize it had been me doing the screaming. He turns away and goes back to maniacally yelling about interplanetary warfare, then about war breaking out between Puerto Rico and El Barrio.

"¡Guerra entre Puerto Rico y El Barrio!"

What? War had broken out between Puerto Rico and El Barrio. My brain tries to sort out all that's happening, with ideas falling into place like balls in a pinball machine. There's no danger. Ha-ha! What he is saying is funny, and I remind myself it's Sunday after Christmas and we are going to El Barrio to visit Grandmother.

We pile into the car.

"Hey, Pops, how come you never go to church?" I ask.

"Because when Jesus walked the earth He stole chickens just like the rest of us."

"Hey, Ma, how come you don't go to church every Sunday?"

"I don't have to go. Jesus understands that I'm a poor working mother."

"How come we ate meat last Friday?"

"Because Jesus understands that I'm a poor working mother."

By that time we are crossing the Willis Avenue Bridge. We get a parking spot right in front of Grandmother's on 111th Street.

"Linda keeps your grandmother's house sparkling like a mirror!" says Ma as we go up the brownstone steps into the apartment—and even as we enter, Uncle Ángel's wife, Linda, is polishing a table.

"¡Hola!" she says in a musical voice that puts Snow White tidying up after the Seven Dwarfs into my mind. She is so cheerful and gay I think I see golden sparkles in the wake of her cleaning cloth. Her children, Evelyn and Peter, are such perfect mirror images of each

other they might be twins, but I know they are not. My aunt La Boba hugs me as my father, bowing his head, says to Grandmother, *"Échame la bendición."* She blesses him and he barely acknowledges his brother Ángel, who ignores him as well.

"Sooonnniiiaaa," Uncle Ángel says with a grin, giving me a Shirley Temple doll. He works in a toy store and gives me a Shirley Temple doll every year. Still, my heart almost stops it is so beautiful. *"¡Felicidades!"* he says. But before I can think what to say, Virginia, a half sister of Pops and Uncle Ángel, breezes in.

"What are you doing cleaning on Sunday?" she chastises Linda. "It's the day of the Lord!"

"We made such a mess with Christmas . . ." says Linda lamely, putting away her magic cleaning cloths. "I thought . . ." But she is cut off by Virginia's holiness.

"It's a day to relax and be thankful for all the good He has done for us."

"Sí . . ."

Ma makes believe she is not in the room and Pops decides to step out for a minute. My doll's beautiful blonde curls mesmerize me.

"Sonia . . ."

The curls are thick and springy.

"Sonia . . ."

I finally realize Virginia is talking to me and I stare at her.

"Have you accepted Jesus Cristo into your heart?"

My heart? I look at Ma.

"Come to Sunday school for a little while. I was just on my way."

"School?" I thought we were supposed to rest today.

"Come, come with me!"

I look at Ma, who does nothing, leaving me hanging out in the wind.

49

"I'll have her back before *la comida*!" And Virginia starts to help me on with my coat. My doll's head gets caught in the sleeve.

"Put her down. She'll be here when you get back." And I am whisked away, abandoning Shirley Temple on the sofa with her legs up in the air.

I end up at a storefront church down the street. There is nothing pretty or dark and scary like at Our Lady of Victory Church. I take my seat with a bunch of other kids. Virginia and the other woman running the church look alike in their plainness. Neither wears makeup; both wear long skirts and ugly shoes. Why don't they wear sexy shoes like Iris, or even shoes like my own ma's pointy ones? They give us paper and crayon. I decide to draw a princess and just when I'm getting to drawing in a golden crown Virginia asks us to put down our crayons. She says it's time to confess our sins. One kid after another gets up and tells everyone what rotten kids they are. When it's my turn I just sit in my chair.

"Come, Sonia, accept Christ into your heart."

I don't make a move.

"It's time to tell your sins."

I sit there and recite my sins in my head in case God's really listening. I don't like this woman. I don't like the gold in her teeth or her dry chapped lips, and that she doesn't wear nail polish, or tweeze her eyebrows, or smear red *colorete* on her cheeks like women are supposed to do. I especially don't like how "good" she is.

"Sonia . . . ?"

I make my face stone and still, like my dolls.

Finally she gives up and takes me back to Grandmother's, where my beautiful doll greets me. Later, on our way home, I tell Ma about what happened.

"You did the right thing. Catholics confess to priests and that's it." And I can tell from the way she said it that she doesn't like Virginia, either, but the whole thing makes her decide that I should finally become a full member of the Catholic Church.

Two weeks later she grabs my birth certificate and takes me to the parish of Our Lady of Victory Church on Webster Avenue. We knock on the parish house door and an old, dusty, papery-white woman answers the door and I know she is Irish.

"Yes?"

She looks like she has a toothache or maybe it just pains her to look at us. Ma presents my birth certificate and says she wants to sign me up. We wait in a neat room with dark furniture and a reddish rug and a big green plant and wooden bookcases, and as we sit I notice that the plant is dusty, as is every other thing in the room.

After a few minutes the old Irish maid is back, and she escorts us into Father Fitzgerald's office. I catch a glimpse of him before he sees us and he is holding his big, bony head in his hands and looking as sad as the Virgin Mary's statue does holding her dead son in the church. There are shafts of light coming in behind him through the stained glass windows, dense with specks of dust flying all around, and I wonder about a priest who is so sad in a place that is so neat and dusty.

Father Fitzgerald comes out of his depression long enough to sign me up for classes. The next Tuesday he picks us Catholic kids up at school for religious instruction, which is supposed to be from two forty-five to three thirty. We get to the church at three and before we know it it's three thirty and time to go home. Still, Father Fitzgerald is never in a hurry. He is like a tall, skinny stick in a skirt that we run out in front of and in back of and all around, like he is a maypole and we are holding ribbons attached to the top of his head. Sometimes we make him laugh and he is not so sad.

Our teacher is Sister Trinitos and she gets us ready for our first communion by telling us all this other stuff besides the one about babies in mangers that I've learned from songs. She says the Father and the Son and the Holy Ghost are one thing, not three things standing next to each other, or on top of each other's heads, but one thing. I am more interested in seeing if she is bald behind her wimple, and fantasize what she'd look like in a dress with a bra underneath until she talks about "original sin." She says that means that though babies look cute outside, inside they are stained black with original sin until they are baptized. That doesn't seem fair: to be marked with somebody else's sins and labeled a sinner before you even have the fun of doing anything bad yourself. I see older kids getting ready to be baptized so I know their insides are black, though they look okay to me.

I try to understand but I can't.

CHAPTER 6

Hunger Camp

S ummer. Ma is the only mother who looks like somebody died. The school has convinced her to let me go away to a Police Athletic League camp for a week, and I can't wait to get away from home. Port Authority Bus Terminal is crammed with kids and parents. Some kids have their things in backpacks or suitcases and even just plain paper bags. My suitcase is brown cardboard with satiny pockets inside.

Ma doesn't even smile when I get on the bus. I'm afraid she's changed her mind about letting me go. I thought she was happy she wouldn't have to worry about babysitting for a week—but now I think she is sorry. Too late! I'm going!

I fall asleep and after four hours wake up when we stop. My sick tooth has leaked and there is wetness down my shirt. Wiping my chin with the back of my arm I gasp at the wildness of where we've come to. There is no lawn like Crotona Park, only really tall trees so close together only strips of light come through. Teachers called counselors greet the bus and they divide us into groups of four. The counselors look like they could all be sisters, cream-colored girls with light-brown hair wearing beige pants and green boots and white shirts. Our counselor is named Lynn and she has long, thick hair and I think they must all have boyfriends.

We head toward the tents in the distance. There are short winding paths so the place looks like a little village in the woods. We don't speak but all four of us campers peek at each other when we can. There's a brown-haired girl with a big nose, there's a black girl with a pointy nose, there's me, and there's a super-skinny girl with hair so blonde it looks as white as her skin. The tents have wooden floors, canvas roofs, and no bathrooms. Before we even put our suitcases down the big-nosed girl has to go to the bathroom.

"Where do we go?" she asks.

"Right this way, ladies," says Lynn.

She shows us to a row of closets with seats with holes in them! "Just do your business in there and don't even worry about flushing." She grins. "This is called an outhouse," she says, and all us girls fall over laughing.

When we are back in the tent we have to say where we are from.

"Bronx," I say.

"Brooklyn," says the black girl.

"Queens," says the brown-haired girl.

"Staten Island," says the white girl.

We pick out our bunks. The minute the brown-haired girl puts her pink suitcase on a bunk, the girl from Staten Island runs over to it and puts her paper bag of clothes on it.

"I want to sleep in this one!" she screeches.

"But I already picked this one," says the big-nosed brown-haired girl.

"I don't care, I want it!"

Lynn comes in before a fight breaks out. She takes the blonde girl outside and talks to her. The next day the angry white-haired girl finds a bullfrog and puts it in a jar. It is so loud it fills the tent with its croaking.

"I can't sleep!" screams the big-nosed brown-haired girl.

All the girls are afraid of it. Again, the camp counselor comes into the tent. She picks up the jar.

"I want my frog!" screams the angry white girl.

Lynn takes the croaking frog and the screaming girl out of the tent. The girl comes back with an empty jar and an angry look on her face.

One day the mail comes and all the girls, except the angry white girl and me, get boxes of chocolates, or crackers, and funny cards from home. Every girl who got a package begins to cry. The angry white girl and I are confused. Shouldn't *we* be crying because we *didn't* get anything?

"Why do they cry?" I ask a counselor.

"Because they are homesick."

"What's 'homesick'?"

The counselor takes a moment before she answers. "It means the packages they've received have reminded them of home and they miss being there."

The angry white girl and I look at each other and I know what we are both thinking. Why would anybody want to be home? After dinner, at night, we all sit around the campfire and sing the song "If I Had a Hammer."

It's the most beautiful song I've ever heard. What a great idea, to sing about "danger" and "justice" and "love between my brothers and my sisters, all over this land"—though I can't say I really "love" my brother and my sister—maybe my sister but not my brother. Every night we sing this really sad song that reminds me of songs I've heard in war movies when somebody dies. But it's a good sad, the kind of sad that makes you think of things, not the kind of sad that chokes you.

We are asked to name our tents and we decide to call ourselves the Bears Tent. The counselors ask for suggestions for names for their tent. "How about the Deer Tent?" says one girl. "Or the Tree Tent?" says another. But I think of how the counselors look like princesses in a fairy tale—and that I'm sure they have boyfriends.

"How about the Love Tent?" I say.

"Yes, perfect," says Lynn.

I am so happy they liked my idea.

I love everything about camp, especially the swimming on my back.

"Legs up, arms up, and sweep the water away. Legs up, arms up, and sweep the water away." I do as I'm told and it works. Yippee! We go on a scavenger hunt. One of the items we have to find is a four-leaf clover.

"What the fuck!" screams the white girl when we find out four-leaf clovers are really hard to find. "That's not fair!"

We have relay races and get to toss a ball and have art class where we usually have our food, which is great, even though I never get enough to eat. The milk is creamy and a beautiful color white in a shapely pitcher. The only days I am really, really hungry as opposed to just a little hungry are Sundays when it is the cook's day off. On those days we have the beautiful milk and donuts for breakfast. When I see kids at other tables not drinking all the milk I ask Lynn for it.

"You guys having that milk . . . ?" Lynn asks.

Suddenly all the kids at the table with the extra milk get thirsty and suck it all up.

"Sorry," says Lynn, patting my leg.

But I forget my hunger when we sing songs around the campfire about an old lady who swallowed a fly, chariots swinging low, and even Greensleeves, whatever they are. I always liked the music my family played and sang, but that was a part of me, like breathing. This new music and words is outside of me. I *decide* to like it, and suddenly I wonder what other things outside of me I'll like.

The morning of our last day the counselor comes in to check our bunks. My pillow has yellow streaks all over it.

"It's from a tooth," I tell her. "That always happens."

She looks at me very closely before saying, "I think you should ask your mother to take you to the dentist."

"But it doesn't hurt yet," I tell her.

"Still—maybe you should go before it starts to hurt."

Lynn doesn't say anything else. She just throws the stained pillow-case with the other dirty things I am to take home.

Ma gasps the minute she sees me step off the bus at Port Authority. "What happened to you?"

"The counselor says you should take me to the dentist."

"You are so skinny!"

"What?"

"Skinny, and you are covered in bumps and cuts and scratches!"

"Did you know that four-leaf clovers hardly exist?"

"*AveMaríaPurísima.*"

"I learned how to swim . . ."

"What kind of camp was that, anyway?"

"And we went on something called a scavenger hunt . . ."

"Starvation camp?"

"No—scavenger hunts and . . ."

"You'll never go away to camp again! ¡Se acabó!"

And we go back to the boring Bronx where Aurea has to take care of Joe and me for the rest of the summer.

Splat! Aurea is flinging oatmeal at my face. Splat! Here comes another one! But she misses and the oatmeal lands on my neck. She is feeding Joe, and in the meantime aims food at me. I don't like being the target but at least I'm being looked at. Soon she gets tired of that game.

"Clean up," she yells. "We're going someplace."

"Where?"

"Just clean up!"

I clean up as she struggles helping Joe with his shoes.

"Where are we going?"

"We are going to buy a giant record!" Suddenly she is so excited her eyes are bright.

"Where do they have that?"

"Way downtown around First Avenue where I used to live—and what do you think about a giant square french fry?

"A what?"

"A giant square french fry! That comes with or without mustard."

"I don't know . . ."

"You'll see," she teases.

I can't imagine this food. We get on the train and sit on the woven rattan seats or hang from the leather straps all the way to Orchard Street.

"Don't stare at the people when we get there," she says.

But it's hard to take my eyes off the men all dressed in black with long curls falling down in front of their ears and long, white, thin strings hanging from underneath their shirts. We go into a dark store. There are barrels of more kinds of pickles than I ever even knew existed. Aurea asks for an extra-sour one for her and a regular one for Joe and me. She picks out two of the potato squares that are called knishes; the one with mustard is hers, and we find a park bench to eat them on. The food is wondrous. Then we go into a record store and buy a huge record called LP for long playing. Imagine that! Twelve songs on a record is like magic. Back on the train the newness of camp and those people and the knish makes me bold enough to ask her a question.

"Hey, Aurea, what does that say?"

"What?"

I point to all the ads in the train.

"All that up there, on the signs. What does it all say?"

But she has grown tired of taking care of two little kids, I think, because she switches.

"Oh . . . why don't you try reading them yourself? Can't you read yet? Christ."

Now this idea makes me stop. I have only read *Dick and Jane* books out loud in school with the rest of the class, the teacher insisting we all stay on the same page. I always *wanted* to read on to see what Dick and Jane did next, but was afraid to peek until the teacher said it was okay. So I'd count the windowpanes, or watch the leaves switching around outside until everyone in the class caught up with me. Now Aurea is telling me to read all by myself.

I look at the letters in the signs and in one split second the words fall into place and I am reading. I'm reading! I read, "For a smooth taste smoke Chesterfield cigarettes." "Don't eat that cake, light up instead." "Most doctors agree Bayer aspirin will make your headache go away." "Winston tastes good like a cigarette should." I focus on a picture of three pretty girls. "Arlene Singer—Brooklyn. Danette Di Napoli—Manhattan. Kersey Ann O'Reilly—the Bronx. Vote for Miss Rheingold Beer today."

"Hurry up!" We have gotten to our stop. "What's the matter with you?"

But I don't say anything to Aurea. I can read and I don't want anyone to know about my secret weapon, and suddenly I can't wait for summer to end and second grade to begin.

"Wake up!" says Ma. "Or you'll be late for school."

Yippee, another school day. Right away I knew I was the smartest girl in class. My penmanship was perfect. I wrote in the lines. I always raised my hand and had the right answer, which means I got to clean the erasers and run errands for the teacher. "What's wrong with you? Go brush your teeth!"

I brush my teeth while singing a commercial I'd seen on TV: "You'll wonder where the yellow went when you brush your teeth with Pepsodent!"

"What are you doing in there? Hurry up! Get dressed! I have to take Joe to the sitter's house before work. Put your socks on! Get your sweater."

Get my sweater? I get an idea to make Ma laugh. I'll go in the closet to get my sweater and make believe I have fallen asleep! Ma will wonder where I am and look in the closet and laugh at how funny my sleepiness is—she will giggle as hard as she does when she watches Jackie Gleason on the TV show *The Honeymooners*.

I get to the closet and close my eyes and wait for her to come and find me. But before I know it . . .

"What are you doing? *¡AveMaríaPurísima! PACIENCIA.*"

. . . I really *did* fall asleep!

She is angry and spreads her fingers out and up in front of her face while saying *"Paciencia"* with such force I think, this time, she's actually going to touch the sky with her fingertips. She practically tosses me a cup of milky sweet coffee and a piece of Italian bread with butter and sends me to school with Genoveva. Damn.

But the sight of a rock I dream of climbing makes me forget my troubles. We pass it every day on my way to school and every day I wonder about climbing it. It is almost half a block long and reaches way up into the sky, and I'm sure that before it was covered with broken bottles, crumpled paper bags, dog doo-doo, and sticky white balloons, dinosaurs climbed it, reaching to eat the leaves on the trees that grew on top. The mountain of rock seems taller and my desire grows bigger each time I pass it.

That morning, I get ahead of Genoveva and figure I can climb to the top before she catches up with her slow-moving, nose-picking, stopping-to-talk-to-whomever-will-talk-to-her way of walking. I run to the top but just when I am about to take a peek at the whole wide world she notices.

"*¡Muchacha . . . !*"

Too late—she is upon me just before I reach the top.

"*¡Véngase!*"

Too bad. Not today. I climb down and trudge to school, but my mood is immediately lifted by the sight of my new friend Marion Uble. She has a white-blonde pixie hairdo and white, white skin and I love her as we jump rope facing each other.

Johnny over the ocean

Johnny over the sea

Johnny broke a bottle and he blamed it on me.

I told Ma, Ma told Pa

Johnny got a beating and a ha ha ha

Johnny jump on one foot, one foot, one foot

Johnny jump on two foot, two foot, two foot . . .

Then the rope gets tangled and we trip all over each other and laugh. Running inside when the bell rings we get to our desks and compare penmanship papers. We are both perfect. Yesterday she taught me a way of counting by marking dots on the paper, which was really the same as counting my fingers, but I didn't say anything. At the end of the day when her skinny, frizzy-blonde-haired mother picks her up and Genoveva picks me up I feel bad that my own ma has to work and can't be there.

When we get to the outcropping Genoveva says she has to stop off in a store. I see my chance and I take it. Up I go and make it to the top. It's all different but the same from up here. Oh my God, can that be Crotona Park I see way over there? The rooftops are all connected to one another . . . maybe that's my friend Marion Uble's house? She lives on Fulton Avenue right across the street from Crotona Park . . . if that's her building, which is connected to another building, which is connected to another and another and is finally connected to mine . . . we might actually live in the same building. I mean—if being connected made you one . . . can't you say it's just one big building that we all live in? I think so. Oh my God! I think I see her yellow hair and her red coat. Yes, it's her and her mother getting home! I'll wave! "Marion!"

Then I hear Genoveva shriek.

"Get down. You going to break your head; I'm going to tell your mami."

Ma never hit me, or slipped her *chancletas* off her feet to throw at me the way other mothers did, but she *was* angry with me for falling asleep in the closet. Back at her house Genoveva fixes me the can of Franco-American Ravioli my mother had left for me.

"Eat that and just sit quietly until your mother comes home!" she says, plopping it in front of me. Though I'm hungry and there is never enough food I eat slowly, wondering what my mother will say . . . but now I feel tired and stretch my arm out on the table and rest my head . . . and from this angle . . . I notice that the . . . the ravioli looks like a cracker. Was a ravioli really two wet saltines stuffed with meat and pressed together along the sides with a fork? Looks that way . . .

I fall asleep and wake to my mother calling to me from the door. *"Véngase."*

Disoriented, cheek stuck to the plastic tablecloth with spit, I disengage and go to her. She looks happy and pretty again, like she always looks after a day out of the house. I get a big smile and hug.

"She went all the way to the top of the rock. She could've broken her neck!"

I push my head into my body like a turtle. But my mother says, *"¿Quién sabe?* Maybe she's going to grow up to be an explorer."

Me? An explorer? I immediately change the direction my head was going in so that when my mother reaches out her hand to pat it, I stand so much taller I am able to meet her halfway.

"There are three kinds of people in the world," says Mrs. Whitman, the teacher, banging on a diagram of world populations with a pointer. It is Brotherhood Week and she is teaching us about all the people in the world we should like. "Now listen," she adds, glaring, then scratching her white, patchy elbows. Bits of dry skin snow down onto her belly as the pointer jabs around crazily. "The three kinds of people are white, yellow, and black."

Marion and I look at each other and at everybody else. She looks embarrassed that she is the only one mentioned in the list of possible humans. Juan has straight hair and creamy skin and Lourdes has browner skin and curly hair. Juan raises his hand.

"What about brown people? Aren't there brown people?"

Mrs. Whitman expands with righteous indignation at the nerve of him asking a question and she sputters, "No, there are no such things as brown people."

Juan looks straight ahead and mutters something. Mrs. Whitman flies to his side, pointer held high in the air.

"What? What did you say?"

He cowers, then whispers, "Nothing."

And she laughs, saying smugly, "I didn't think so."

And then one kid laughs, and then another, then another, until the whole class laughs at Juan.

"Moving on," says Mrs. Whitman. "There are also three classes of people: rich, middle class, and poor . . ."

I wonder where my family and I stand. Surely we are in the middle class. Poor people sleep in the street like Moncho, outside of Don Joe's bodega, and never have anything to eat like those people in Puerto Rico who live over shit rivers in El Fanguito. We sleep in beds and eat something every night. At two forty-five it's my turn to help Mrs. Whitman with her outside shoes. They are black and thick with a strap that holds in her rebellious feet.

"Not too tight," she scolds painfully. I look up at her.

"Mrs. Whitman, am I in the middle class?"

"Oh . . ." She gasps, annoyed. "No, you are poor. Very poor, just like everybody else in this school," she adds, pointing to her shoe. "Now loosen that strap; you've made it much too tight."

That night I tell my mother what Mrs. Whitman had said and I ask if we are poor or not.

"We're doing all right," she sniffs, turning her face away.

The school year goes quickly. It's finally summer again and Marion is all set to come to the lake with us. Marion's mother uses a lot of "r"s when she tells us that it's okay for Marion to come. And it is a special trip because we are going with Caguas *y* Paula and their eight children.

"Why is he called Caguas?" I ask Ma.

"Why do you think? Because that's where he is from."

"Is his wife, Paula, from a place called Paula?"

"No, that's just her name."

Caguas is white and regular size and Paula is big and round with really dark skin and they love each other so much they have eight kids that are all a color between them. I like to go to their apartment because they are always laughing and being nice to each other, even though their kitchen has such greasy walls they glisten. Going to the beach with them means that there will be lots of roast pork, and rice and beans, and whole watermelons! All the big kids help the little kids as they walk in size places carrying their picnic stuff to the car.

When we get to Lake Welch, Marion and I head for the water right away and after playing in the sand and getting wet again we go up to, we think, Paula for a towel.

"Paula, ¿dame una toalla, por favor?" I say.

And the big, round, dark woman turns around to me slowly, and smiles, and says in a warm, syrupy voice, "Chile, I don't know whatchu sayin'."

Marion and I back off, looking for our own group, but I keep wondering how it was possible that I could I have thought that that black woman was Paula. Paula is Puerto Rican and everyone knows that Puerto Ricans aren't black. Right? Later, after watermelon, Marion and I go back to the water's edge.

"¡Muchachas! ¡Sálganse del sol!"

Ma wants us to get out of the sun, Marion because she was turning too red and me because I was turning too dark and we wouldn't want anyone to mistake me for being a Negro.

CHAPTER 7

Family Mood Swings

B iting into the food feels like I am eating my own tongue. But it's not my tongue—it's some poor cow's tongue I am cramming down my throat. I am home with my father because I am sick and he is not on a roofing job because it's raining. We eat the disgusting food he loves—*cuchifritos,* pickled pigs' ears and tongue, and *morcilla,* or blood sausage. I eat it so he'll like me better, carefully chewing around the one hair the cook missed on the sow's ear.

The phone rings and I know it's his boss because my father suddenly gets nervous and forgets how to speak English. When he has to write something down he panics because there is no handy pencil and he digs around all the kitchen drawers, reaching as far as the phone cord lets him until he finds a discarded Maybelline eyebrow pencil of Ma's, to finally write some information on the wall. Then he surprises me: "Let's go—we gotta go to Yonkers to *la casa del* boss."

I put on two sweaters because I'm cold even though it's summer and we drive to his boss's house in Yonkers, and when we get there I think it's worth it because I have never seen such a beautiful house except maybe for Dick and Jane's house in my school reader. Big bushes heavy with pink flowers caress our car as we turn into the driveway. My father rings the doorbell and a tall white man with long, stringy arms, blond hair, and wet blue eyes answers.

"Chico, come on in."

Chico? Who is "Chico"? I look to see if there is someone behind us. My father is called "Bonifacio Manzano," or "Pepe." I have never heard "Chico."

The man eyes me, smiling. "How come you're not in school?"

I look at my father.

"Oh, this is my daughter, Sonia. She don't feel well."

"Well, come on in, Sonia," says the boss.

I walk into the living room and sink into the carpet up to my ankles.

"Would you like a cookie?" It's the boss's wife, who looks exactly like her husband except her lips are covered with coral-orange lipstick, with a little lipstick on her yellow teeth, too. Her long toes are painted the same color orange, and are so trapped in white, shiny leather sandals they cross like fingers wishing good luck. My words stick in my throat, even if I did know how to answer the cookie question.

She laughs and shows me into a living room full of big plants, where I sit in a chair so soft I watch my dark thin legs sink in until they are almost gone. My father and his boss go through sliding glass doors just like people do in the movies, onto a patio where the boss sits as my father stands. *How come we don't live like this?* I think. *Are we not in the same world? How can they work together and live so differently from each other?* I watch the boss talk and my father smile, trying to keep up. They come back into the room where I can hear them but my father is less animated now, watching his boss carefully, and giving him the expected reaction almost moments before he needs to. By the time we get home I feel worse, with feverish thoughts on fire in my head. How come my father is so scared? Why was he tripping and falling over every broken English word that came out of his mouth? I go straight to my bed to lie down and the next thing is Ma, purse dangling from her arm, feeling my face then pulling her hand back because I am so hot. My throat is on fire, but my head is in a wonderful place because I have Ma all to myself. She wraps me up in clean, dry sheets, slathers me with mustard plasters, gives me soft foods like mashed potatoes and chicken noodle soup as the days go by.

"Ma, my head is part of a calendar like in a movie showing time going, going . . ."

"¿Qué . . . ?"

She looks alarmed so I don't go on. How can I explain that I feel like I'm in a black-and-white movie, the part where they show time passing, with pages of a calendar blowing away? My head is one of the calendar pages about to go into the future or back into the past and I am not afraid. Ma wrings her hands like actress Joan Crawford.

That night I sleep until the whiskey smell of my father wakes me, but I don't move in case I am still in a movie. He sits by my bed and begins to cry. I peek and can see half his face in shadow, and as he tries to hold it all in, the sobs burst forth, faster and harder. He heaves great gulps of sad air, until he can't anymore.

Many weeks later when there is no work for a long time because it's rained so much he comes home in a black mood as Joe and I finish dinner.

"Go to bed."

"But it's still daylight . . . ?"

"Don't you talk back to me! Go to bed! Both of you! Now!"

We go to bed but Joe and I can't sleep on account of it is still bright outside.

"Hey, Joe," I whisper, "want to play trampoline?" Joe never talks but he wants to jump. We jump a little at first, then higher, and higher, and higher, and higher until my father gallops into the room like the horse Fury on TV. His ears back, his nostrils flared, his eyes wild. Tall and muscular as a comic-book avenger, his stance wide, his head squared, belt held high in his hand, he lets it unfurl on my legs.

Later after crying until my eyes are sticky shut and I sleep, my thigh goes through a transformation. A magnificent bruise appears by morning, outstanding in size and color with rings of black, purple, red, and yellow.

All day, looking at my prize, I wait, looking out the window, imagining being in the spotlight of my mother's eyes, the center of her attention, even getting sympathetic sighs, like she got from neighbors when she was hit. But Aurea comes home in an unexpectedly great mood—smiling, even. She plays Nat King Cole singing "Love Is the Thing" before putting on a pot of beans to simmer. Cole's sweet honey voice and the burbling beans warm up the apartment. Aurea drapes a pink scarf over our lamps, making soft light. Her activities divide my attention between the atmosphere and my thigh.

"Wanna play cards?" she says.

I can't believe my ears. Playing cards with my sister in the middle of this suddenly heavenly apartment is almost more than I can bear. Only friends play cards. I want to jump up but my leg is sore. We play a round of cards and grin at each other and it feels so delicious I want to share more.

"You want to see something?" I tease.

"What?"

"Look."

I show her my thigh—she gasps, her face turning dark. Standing up, agitated, she begins to pace, flicking the deck of cards from one hand to the other.

"What's the matter?" I say, stunned by this quick turn.

When she doesn't answer, I wonder what I have done wrong. How had I managed to ruin the moment? I have spoiled everything! How can I have been so stupid! We were playing cards! I want to play cards! What about the cards? But she doesn't want to play cards anymore. She wants to take me to the police station.

"Put these clean panties on," she commands.

"Can we still play cards?" I ask, slipping in my sore leg first.

She doesn't answer me. Our game has changed to scary. We are on a secret mission now. Ma comes home and I know to be silent. My sister says nothing important and tells Ma we are going to buy some candy.

But my sister's timing is off. We run into my father downstairs.

"Where do you two think you are going?" he shouts.

"We're going to get some candy . . ."

He must suspect something because he says, "No, you're not. Get upstairs, both of you!"

They argue. Flor comes out of Don Joe's bodega to watch. Don Joe himself comes out and tries to interfere. One of the red-haired Cabeza men sits in his windowsill in an undershirt, his feet on Don Joe's awning, watching us like some red, hairy gorilla. The whole neighborhood is watching. I scream for Ma, who finally and painfully looks down on the show from the window.

Maybe he pushes Aurea toward the building—I don't know, but she leaps up at him, shoving him back with all her might, and I feel small on the sidewalk and I am pretty sure I hate him.

But something good happens. Aurea so detests being at home that she goes to the Fenway movie theater every night and takes me with her. She loves the movies, and we are safe in the darkness, and I give her sidelong glances each time I want to see joy.

Soon there is work again and my father is out of the house and there is no school so I have to stay at a neighbor's for the day. She is a square block of a woman in a housedress we don't know very well but she lives right next door; and it won't be a regular thing anyway. She greets me wearing her husband's hand-me-down shoes, her hair in pigtails. I watch her tuck her two babies into bed for their naps, then stand around waiting to be told what to do.

"You just sit in that chair," she tells me, pointing to a chair against the wall that I go sit in. I can just see into the bedroom where the babies are.

"Do not move from that chair." She smiles, getting into the bed with them.

I sit in the chair and wait. There is a clock and I'm happy that it ticks and tocks because it gives me something to listen to. The train zooms by outside. Smiling inside, I tell myself this babysitter is better than the one with the twelve-year-old son who always wanted to play "getting married in the Old West," which I liked to play because I got to make believe I was wearing a wedding dress and being helped into a wagon by my new husband—but I didn't like it when he snuck his tongue into my mouth. At least at *this* sitter's house all I have to do is sit in a chair.

I hear soft snoring. My feet don't quite reach the floor so I make believe I am a ballerina and I go back and forth along the length of the chair on my tippy-toes. The dance I make up is very long and I add to it by making believe I am leaping out of the chair, landing on my toes, and sliding back to my place as smoothly as if the floor were slick as ice. My dance is long and I go through it several times but they still don't wake up.

My arms dangle at my sides and I brace them against the chair and lift my whole body up. Up and down, and up and down. I could be an acrobat in the circus, and in my mind I am flipping through the air, demonstrating great feats of strength and endurance like I saw in a favorite movie, *Trapeze*. I even lift my feet straight out in front of me, and notice I am no longer wearing imaginary ballet slippers but imaginary nude-colored slippers and fishnet tights with tiny bits of glitter on them. Suddenly the babysitter stirs and I leap with joy and hope nap time is over and I can get out of this chair, but she just peers at me with one eye and goes back to sleep. Sinking back, I let my head drop and I listen to myself breathe.

Finally she is up and I am released and home with yet another neighbor on this day of relay-race babysitters watching over me until Ma gets home. I am so bored I could cry until Cousin Eddie comes over and my feeling is mixed—glad to see him but jealous of the freedom he has to come and go. Immediately he points out a pile of oak tag paper peeking out of Aurea's room.

"Look at the paper," he says

I look at it but know not to touch it. Aurea would kill me.

"You can have it, you know," he says.

"No . . ."

"Yes," he insists. "You can draw something."

I think of all the things I would draw: a house, with a tree and the sun shining down, birds flying, kids playing.

"Look, I'll even get you some crayons." And he goes into my sister's room and comes out with a box full of crayons. I can't believe it.

"That's Aurea's and I'm not supposed to touch it," I say. But it would be so wonderful to touch it.

"She said it was okay."

"What?"

"Really, I just saw her and she said it was okay to have the paper and crayons so you can draw."

Suddenly Little Eddie, the room, the sounds, everything disappears. The only things in the world are the oak tag, the crayons, and me. Opening the package I take one sheet of paper out and spread it on the floor. It is a beautiful, delicious cream color with a little bit of shine. What can I draw? Should I draw a mermaid or a flamenco dancer? I think this project deserves some thought.

But suddenly my sister swoops in.

"What are you doing?" she yells.

I'm dumbfounded.

"You can't have that!"

"But Eddie said . . ."

"I don't care what Eddie said. That paper is expensive. Are you crazy!" And she snatches up the oak tag and crayons and storms into her room, slamming the door.

A white-hot fury washes over me, making me pick up a piece of wood with a nail in it that my father had left lying around and fling it at Eddie—the nail catches him at the shins, piercing his freedom, almost fixing him down to the ground as steadfastly as I felt nailed.

He howls in pain, and limps around as my sister pulls the nail out, all the while yelling at my meanness, even as she runs into the bathroom to get the brownish-red Mercurochrome that makes him howl even louder when she swabs it on. I don't cry. I just look out the window until the white-hot fury fades and I stop trembling.

The next day Little Eddie comes over. He smiles and laughs like I hadn't thrown a board with a nail in it at him. Once again, he finds everything I do hilarious and good and I am not ugly and mean after all, and before I know it I'm riding on the handlebars of his ten-speed bicycle. We fly down Crotona Parkway onto Third Avenue—I am scared, but his laughter in my ear makes it a good kind of scared and as we fly faster and faster under the El, the slats of sun coming through the tracks are like what I'll know much later to be a strobe effect, but at that perfect moment of power and freedom I'm sure that no one in the whole world could possibly be as happy as me.

CHAPTER 8

Queen for a Day

Our teacher Mr. Gitterman is reading to us from *Charlotte's Web*. It's a magic book that makes everyone settle down, even the kids who can never sit still. Marion cups her chin in her hands and twirls her hair. I forget about myself and sit with my knees apart and my mouth open.

Mr. Gitterman is all one color of sand as he sits on a student desk facing us. He reads slowly, letting the words wash over us like rain, sometimes stopping to look past us and out the window, as if he might be thinking about something that had happened to him. Sometimes he scratches his ankle.

Even when we know that he will soon stop because it's almost time to get our coats and go home, we wait, long and quietly, so we can squeeze a few more sentences out of him. One day we groan so loudly when he stops he tells us that our parents should read to us every day, just like he does.

"Mr. Gitterman says you should read to me every day," I say to Ma later.

"Like I don't got enough to do?"

"That's what he said."

"We don't have any books," she says.

I ask him the next day, "What do we do if we don't have any books?"

"You don't need to have books. Your parents can just tell you stories about their lives."

I wait until Ma is dyeing her gray hair before I ask her for a true story about her life because she has to sit perfectly still as she pours black Loving Care hair dye onto her head and cover it over with a clear plastic bag. She sits with a wad of tissue to keep the black goop from dripping down onto her face.

"Tell me the story you and Bon Bon were talking about," I say.

She looks at me blankly.

"The story about the guy who threw the coconuts at his wife's head."

"What about him?"

"Did he change?"

"Who?"

"The man who threw coconuts at his wife's head."

"No. He was a mean *sinvergüenza,* and mean, shameless men never change."

"And she never moved out of the way?"

"No."

"Why?"

"Because she was a good person."

"But why does letting someone bounce coconuts off your head make you a good person?"

"She was a good person, not like a person, but like a saint." By this time Ma misses a few drips of dye and begins to resemble Christ wearing His crown of thorns at the church, with blood dripping down His forehead. She leans toward me, raises both eyebrows, and says, "Get it?"

I don't but I want to hear the rest of the story. "What *happened* to her?"

"She took it, and took it, and took it, until her children grew up and saved her by taking her away from him."

I think that by that time the woman probably wouldn't have a head or a body left to take away. My mother lights a Kent cigarette while I think the woman is like Charlotte in *Charlotte's Web*, who mostly suffers for a pig named Wilbur.

"Tell me about your mother," I say. Often I have to light a candle in Abuela's name at church, but all I really know is her name, Encarnación Falcon, and that she died when Ma was five years old.

"Now *she* was a real saint. Poor thing . . . she was so good she died of a broken heart."

"What do you mean?"

"Someday you will understand."

"Tell me now . . ."

"My father broke her heart by having other women, and by the time she had five children she couldn't take it anymore and just died. She left Cristina, Eduardo, and me, Francisco, and Félix. There was one more, Felipe, but he lived such a short time I don't count him. You know, I think she came back for him . . ."

I imagine Encarnación Falcon swooping down from heaven to get her last baby, and telling Ma and her siblings to look out for each other.

"I remember our little *bohío* when she died . . ."

"What's a *bohío*?"

"A little wooden house. It was in Aguas Buenas, full of people crying and drinking rum. There were people from the town, and relatives I didn't know. One of them put his hand inside my dress, and my aunt kept saying, '*¡Cállense la boca!*' and 'Stop crying.' I was all confused and didn't know what was going to happen to us."

"You still had a father, Dionisio," I say.

"He was a man and men didn't take care of children. And anyway, there were five of us and there was no food or money. *Terrible. La pobreza*. He gave us away."

"What? He gave you away?"

"So we could work for people for food. It was the only way."

I think of all the five-year-old kids that I know running around the neighborhood. They couldn't be on their own. One kid is always sticking beans up his nose. My cousin Mickey can't wipe his nose. How would it be if they had to take care of themselves?

Ma continues. "I had to go away with a family that needed me to take care of two babies. They say they could make more money if I took care of the children. But they left me alone in a house full of holes in the floor and under the house were mongoose . . ."

"What's a mongoose?"

"*AveMaríaPurísima!* Like long, skinny rats. And they were wild and screamed from hunger even more than the babies did. I was afraid to go outside. I was supposed to feed the children rice, but I couldn't take the children crying for more rice and the mongooses screaming under the house. I thought they wanted a baby to fall through so they could eat it. So one morning I fed the kids, and I didn't even take my share, and I put some chairs over the holes in the floor and waited until I could jump over the mongooses, and then I ran away to find my father. I found him working at a bakery and I remember the tip of his belt swaying as he made frosting."

How could a man who gave away his children make frosting?

"I just sat in the doorway and waited for him to notice me."

I almost don't want to know but ask anyway. "And then what happened?"

"He found me a place in Fajardo, a town near the beach.

AveMaríaPurísima, that family was crazy. I had to sweep and make sure not even one grain of sand would get in the house. I was afraid they would spackle me into a wall if I missed any."

"You thought they would do that? Really?"

By this time Ma is tired.

"I don't know," she says. "It seemed so . . ." She lights another cigarette and goes on.

"So when I got such a fever I was freezing in the burning sun I ran away again. But I didn't have any shoes that fit so I found a pair that was too big and stuffed them with socks to keep them on and found my Mama Santa . . ."

Another saint?

". . . my mother's mother, who was taking care of the baby, Félix . . ."

"Why didn't she take care of you, too?"

"*Muchacha*, there were too many of us. I walked for miles in those shoes and finally got to her house, but there was nobody home. I took off my shoes and my socks peeled away the first layer of skin on both heels. But I was happy to be able to lean back against the door to let the sun sweat my fever out."

This is like the tropical version of the story of "The Little Match Girl," who had to sell matches on a freezing Christmas Eve or risk being beaten by her father. I think of the Match Girl lighting matches to stay warm, then jump to an image of my poor ma, sick and baking in the sun. I don't know where to put my sadness for my mother. Ma rinses out her hair at the kitchen sink. I watch the black dye swirl around and go down the drain.

Ma suddenly laughs ruefully.

"What?" I ask.

"Months later I had a stomachache. Mama Santa had me drink my baby brother Félix's urine."

"Eeeew! That's disgusting!"

"It made my stomachache go away."

"How?"

"I threw up, and I never complained about an upset stomach again."

I have had enough of true stories.

"Now tell me a made-up story."

"*AveMaríaPurísima*—another one?" Her eyes bug out on purpose, making me laugh as she wraps her head in a towel.

"A woman lives with her four children in Crotona Park and . . ."

"In the winter?"

"Don't interrupt. A woman lives with her four children in Crotona Park in the winter and her husband beats her and beats her until her children grow up and save her. The end."

I don't say anything.

Her made-up story was sad, but not as sad as the real-life story she'd had in Puerto Rico—and the fear and sorrow she must've felt when she was a kid stays with me.

I am watching my favorite show, *Queen for a Day*. "Would you like to be queen for a day?" the announcer asks the contestants at the beginning of each show, and I think, yes, because if anyone qualifies for being queen for a day it's my mother. "Tell us about yourself," the announcer asks a tired-looking white woman. She doesn't look like the white women on *Father Knows Best* or on *The Donna Reed Show*. She looks dumpy. I study her and place my mother between her and television moms. My mother could look beautiful *and* beat-up at the same time.

"We live in Kentucky and my child had polio and can't get around and just when we had saved up enough money to buy a wheelchair my husband lost his job at the coal mine and . . . and . . ."

She can't go on she's crying so much. The announcer pats her on the back.

"Well, do you have any other children?"

"Yes, we have a little girl, four years old . . ."

"Does she have polio?"

The woman is a little shocked at this question. "Why, no . . ."

"Now, you should be thankful for that, shouldn't you be?"

"Yes, I . . ."

He cuts her off. "Why do you think you should be queen for a day?"

"Because my boy . . . has to crawl around the house, pullin' himself on his arms . . . and we could use a wheelchair."

She might win. I think hard. Mothers with crippled kids always get a lot of applause and that's how the winner is chosen, by how much applause they get. But I'm not crippled. Damn.

"Well, that's just fine," says the announcer as he slides over to the next contestant. "Tell us your story."

The next woman says she lost her husband in a mud slide. When he went back into the house to rescue the family dog, the house slid down right out from under him. Husband, house, dog—all lost to her. And now she's been left with four children and wants a washing machine so she can take in laundry.

There are no stories about women who work. My mother works in a sewing factory. At the commercial break I run to the window to look out for her.

A train pulls in and out with no mother, so I run back to the television set and watch the third contestant. She has twins and is pregnant with what may be more. Her husband has run out on her with a country-western singer who was coming through town. Now she has to raise twin two-year-olds, and whatever babies she's carrying. The announcer tells her how lucky she is to be blessed with children.

"What would you like if you were queen for a day?"

"Some clothes for my children . . ."

Okay, now it's getting exciting for me. I see my mother in that category. Not the pregnant or clothes part, but the part about escaping the cruelty of a mean husband. That could work. That woman doesn't even have black-and-blue marks on her. Ma would beat her for sure.

Finally it's time to pick the winner. They bring out an applause meter. The announcer stands over the woman who needs a wheelchair. The audience goes nuts. Their enthusiasm makes the dial go all the way up to ten!

Then he slides over to the woman who wants a washing machine. She gets some applause but not much, just up to number six. Then he slinks over to the contestant who wants clothes. She gets the least amount of applause. He goes back to the wheelchair woman. They pan to the audience going wild, then back to her. Now she *really* starts to cry. I knew it. I knew she was going to be the winner.

I make believe I see them put a crown on my mother's head, and a fur cape like Old King Cole wore, over her shoulders.

Then I make believe they give her everything she wants . . . and more. A washing machine, *and* a refrigerator, pots and pans, dishes. My mother on TV looks dramatic, tears welling in her eyes like an actress in an old movie. I know she would win if she could just get on that show, and that makes me feel good and hopeful because it would be just like TV where everything is fine.

CHAPTER 9

Banishment, Threats, and a Suicide

We are going to church, but my sister heads in the opposite direction.

"Where are you going?" I ask.

"To the park."

She continues across the street to St. Mary's Park. Father Fitzgerald sees me coming.

"Hello, Sonia," he says sadly.

"Hi, Father . . ."

Then he forces a smile and says, *"Buenos días, qué bueno que viniste a la misa hoy,"* and doesn't mind that I laugh at his accent. I go into church adjusting a tissue I have bobby-pinned on my head because I don't have a *mantilla*. The church is dark and somber and beautiful and when the father starts speaking Latin my mind wanders. I wonder what hurts more, the stab wound in Christ's side or the real chip in His plaster toe?

Sister Trinitos had told us of a little girl who loved God so much and prayed so hard at church He finally granted her wish and took her away so she could be with Him in heaven. When Mass was over and everybody got up to leave she just fell over dead like a sack of potatoes.

I start to think that if He could hear her good thoughts, He can probably hear my bad ones—the ones that come into my head the minute I try to stop thinking of them. *Shit! Oh no! Did God hear me think* shit? *Oh fuck. Oh no, now He heard me think* fuck *and . . . that other one. Goddamn it. Great . . . now He heard me think* Goddamn it. *At the rate I'm going, I'm sure to rot in hell. Oh wait, isn't* hell *a bad word, too?* I close my eyes and think that I can't take it anymore and if I am going to die I want to be taken now! So I let every bad word I know float through my mind, in English and Spanish: *carajo, pendejo, coño, hijo de puta, snot!* I open my eyes and see Father Fitzgerald is right near me! He must've heard me, too!

Finally Mass is over and I run away with my life until next week. Gasping for fresh air I find Aurea in the crowd, waiting for me with a smirk on her face. She's always right on time.

"How come you know when to pick me up?" I say.

"When I see all you morons coming out," she answers.

We go home and Ma makes breakfast. Eggs fried in bacon and big cups of coffee, but Ma is so irritated and throws the food around with such disgust, globs of grease fall into the coffee.

"I don't know if we should go," says Ma.

"Why not?" says Pops.

"I don't know . . . so sad . . . Linda gone . . ."

My ears perk up. "What happened to Linda . . . ?"

"Shhh . . ." says Ma.

"Let's go!" my father announces.

"I'm not going," says my sister.

Time stops. Who will win?

"She has to stay here and defrost the refrigerator," says my mother nervously, and it's like a bell ringing at a boxing match. My father and sister go back into their own corners. After that we pile into the car and ride to Grandmother's house.

The house doesn't sparkle anymore. It is neat but dull, and dirt is now embedded in the corners of the kitchen floor. I notice roaches in the cabinets. Were they always there? No one is home but La Boba and Grandmother.

"*Échame la bendición.*" "Pour your blessing on me," says my father, bowing his head. I give the shorter version.

"*Bendición,*" I say to Grandmother.

"*Dios te bendiga,*" she answers solemnly.

After a while my father gets up.

"I have to go see somebody about a job . . . I'll be back soon." He leaves, promising to pick us up later.

"*Perate, perate, perate . . .*" Grandmother starts to motor around the kitchen making coffee. She heats up the milk until it almost boils over, pours it into two cups, and then darkens them with coffee. She and Ma talk and I try to blend into the scenery so I can hear what happened to Linda.

"Linda took off her wedding ring to use Ajax to clean the toilet," begins Grandmother.

"Really . . ."

"*Sí* . . . Virginia saw her without her wedding band. When Ángel came home, Virginia said, '*Ay, Dios mío*—your wife took her ring off to deny her marriage!'"

"Deny her marriage? I thought she took her ring off to clean the toilet!" says Ma.

Grandmother nods but says nothing. I listen to the grandfather clock ticking away in the silence.

"What could Ángel do but throw her out?"

I try to make sense of what they are saying but it's hard.

"Three months later Linda came back with Christmas gifts for Evelyn and Peter."

"*Pobrecita.*"

"Ángel threw the gifts down the steps."

"*Ay, bendito . . .*"

"We never saw Linda again."

They sit quietly for a moment before Grandmother continues. "Then Virginia thought it would be best if Peter lived with her. You know—to help out . . ."

I think the story is so sad and I wonder where my cousin Evelyn is, even as I hear this tale about her mother being banished, like a princess from a castle, and her brother being taken away by the evil witch. But then they go on to talk about another of Pops's brothers.

"What happened to Miguel's wife?"

"*Loca*, Miguel came home and there she was, dead."

"Oh my God . . ."

"Dead with their two children. She dressed them up in white, dragged the cots into the kitchen, lay down with them, and turned on the gas."

"Horrible," my mother agrees.

Later, in our apartment in the Bronx, Ma irons a white shirt for me because I am to be in the color guard in school on Monday. White shirt, blue pleated skirt, and red kerchief must be gotten ready. I watch the hot iron steam away wrinkles and make the shirt smooth and sharp, and the smell of cleanness is good. Ma speaks— her words shooting out like hot chips.

"Linda must have died. What mother would leave her kids on

account of a stupid-ass jealous husband—and poor Miguel's wife? She kept complaining of the beatings Miguel gave her but no one believed her. I would've killed myself, too, if I had married that lunatic."

I go to sleep with banishment in my mind like I had heard it in some fairy tale, not in my own family. And suicide is as far away from me as a story in the *Daily News*—or is it? Ma still hides all the kitchen knives in the oven when it gets dark and my father isn't home yet. Does she think he will stab her? Us? If two of my father's brothers have driven their wives away, could my father somehow cause my own mother's disappearance?

CHAPTER 10

Buried Treasure

We visit Little Eddie and his family in Brooklyn.

"*Bendición,*" I sing out to my uncle as I look for my cousin.

"*Dios te bendiga,*" he replies, but he's really looking at my mother, who wants to know this new way Bon Bon has lost her mind.

"*¿Qué está pasando?*" says Ma.

"*¡Esta mujer se ha vuelto loca!*"

I pass Zoraida curled up in bed on her side with her hands between her knees looking so sorry and lonely. I suppress a desire to throw a comforting blanket on her and go off to find Little Eddie when I hear my mother say, "Gold? In the basement? *¡No me digas!*"

"Yes!"

I find him. We're excited, laughing.

"What's so funny?"

"How should I know?"

We follow everybody down to the basement.

It looks like a Con Ed work site. Bon Bon, wild-eyed, whacks away at a hole in the ground, sure that her next strike will reveal the buried treasure. My mother looks down the hole suspiciously, my uncle Eddie rolls his eyes, and my father grins.

After watching her bring up wet rubble and chunks of concrete for a while, Cousin Eddie and I go upstairs.

"Look, here's what you gotta know . . ." And he beats five counts on his knees. "It's called a *clave* beat."

"A what?"

"A *clave* beat. Now you try it."

I do. And he shows me different accents. We beat different rhythms on our knees until we fall over laughing because we think we are drummers.

"What are you two doing?"

It is my mother checking up on us.

"Come—we have a cup of coffee and then we go . . ."

Bon Bon shakes Zoraida awake.

"Make coffee."

"Leave that child alone," says Ma.

Bon Bon wakes her anyway.

After Zoraida cleans up after us, we gather ourselves to leave but not before I see Bon Bon scurry back to the basement and hear my uncle mutter "Fucking nut" before going back to reading the sports page.

Days later the phone rings. "What?" says Ma. "Spirits made chairs in the basement start spinning around? You think it's a sign to move out and come live near us?"

"I think a clearer 'sign' was probably the landlord seeing the hole she made in the basement," says Aurea. "She's nuts."

But all I can think about is that Little Eddie is going to live near us, and I am so happy I can burst. They move into Bathgate Avenue, so now with Uncle Franco and the cousins already on Fulton Avenue north of me, and Uncle Eddie on Bathgate Avenue south of me, and the Third Avenue El and me in the middle, and family gatherings every Friday, I feel I've had a dream come true.

I'm mooning around the apartment the Friday before Marion Uble's birthday party. I've been thinking about it for weeks, stroking the festive party invitation, gently touching the gaily wrapped box of hankies Ma and I had bought on Bathgate Avenue. Every day I play in my mind how it is going to be when I get there and how Marion will react when she sees my fabulous gift to her.

Soon the uncles arrive with their families. The men drink beer and talk loud, arguing about the best way to fix a car. Little Eddie tries to get my attention, but all I can think about is the party I will go to the next day. Somehow Bon Bon gets wind of it and, like we are friends, she pulls me aside. "Does your father know you are going?" she asks me.

What? I'm speechless. I hadn't thought of him. My mother knew. She helped me pick the present.

"Pepe," I overhear Uncle Eddie say, "if you did that to a car you'd junk it for sure . . ."

"No, I think it would work," Pops says lamely.

"Ask him now," Bon Bon goads. "With all of us here he would never think of saying no to you. Go ahead . . ."

"Naw," scoffs Uncle Frank. "You better leave car fixing to us."

"I used to fix cars in Puerto Rico . . ." says my father, trying to get back in the conversation.

Bon Bon winks at me and gives me encouraging looks.

My father is in the middle of defending himself but I blurt out anyway . . .

"Papi . . . tomorrow is my friend's birthday party . . ."

"*¿Qué . . . ?*" He zeroes in on me.

". . . can I go?"

And he makes a definitive statement no one can argue with: "You are not going to any party . . ."

I can't believe I've heard right! Not going to the party? But I was going to go! I have a present and everything . . . the handkerchiefs. I'm stunned and look to Ma, who turns away. Even Bon Bon looks chastised. In one second—no, less than one second—my world spins from light to darkness and a lump of disappointment lodges in my throat.

The next day I follow Ma around the apartment asking her questions, trying to loosen the lump that won't go away.

"I wonder what they are doing now. Do you think they are playing with her dollhouse? Do you think they are playing pin the tail on the donkey? Is it time for them to cut the cake or open the presents?"

Ma doesn't answer me, and no matter how many questions I ask, the lump does not dissolve—it hardens and turns into a part of me.

CHAPTER 11

Breasts

Suddenly I am old enough to walk around the neighborhood by myself, which is good, except I have to take small, tiresome, budding breasts with me, which is bad. Everybody noticed them before me: the boys who followed me into the water at Crotona Pool to feel them up, the stranger who stared and smiled at me from the train platform in such a familiar way I thought I knew him; even the parks worker stopped picking up litter so he could lick his lips and stare. Every morning I wake up and look around for my new worry before it finds me, and it's my breasts.

It is early September—time to drool over getting new school supplies. Visions of pencil kits and notebooks and erasers dance in my head as the days cool. Too impatient to wait until the weekend when we would shop on Bathgate Avenue, I badger Ma into letting me buy at least one composition notebook at the drugstore.

"It's just downstairs, Ma. I can go by myself."

She says okay and gives me some money.

After I longingly caress the packages of three-by-five cards, the boxes of crayons, and the number-two pencils and notebooks, I pick out a composition notebook and examine it. I never tire of looking at the multiplication table in the back. So neat and even, it never lets you down. I take it up to the pharmacist. He smiles and asks if I want a free box of crayons. Crayons. I think quickly; I don't have any construction paper to draw on, but that's okay, I can figure out how to get that later and I can draw in my notebook in the meantime.

"Yes!" I say. "Thank you."

He comes out from behind the counter, picks up a box from the display, hands it to me, and manages to let his hands stray to my chest, where he fingers my breasts. My grateful feelings for the crayons twist into something else. Then he offers me a giant box of crayons, the kind that has a sharpener built right in, and my mouth waters. I almost stop breathing, deciding what do. Should I let him feel me up for a box of crayons?

A red-faced cop on his beat breaks the devil mood.

"Hey!" he yells, sticking his head in the door and rapping his nightstick on the doorjamb.

The sound of the nightstick sends the rat-faced pharmacist scurrying back behind the counter so fast it is as if he flew. I think of the expression of someone running with "their tail between their legs," because it looks like his pants got sucked right up into his ass. I drag myself up the stairs and enter our apartment with my new notebook pressed against my chest.

"You got it!"

"Huh?"

"*La libreta* . . ."

"Oh yes, the notebook—yes, I got it." That's all I say. I don't want to tell her what happened in case it had, in some way, been my fault, and I want to make sure I will still be allowed to go out.

———

Balancing a covered plate of food, I am careful going up the steps to the cousins' apartment on Fulton Avenue. Mickey and Chaty wrestle in front of the television set. The horizontal hold has been fixed and now it's got color since my uncle has pressed a plastic screen on it that is blue at the top for sky, green at the bottom for grass, and yellow in the middle for air; it kind of works if you are watching a western. Every now and then Mickey manages to sit on Chaty's head and fart.

Uncle Frank and Aunt Iris have a different way of fighting from Ma and Pops. Iris shows her anger by humming a tuneless song as she stares out onto Crotona Park at the trees her sons have managed to destroy, while Uncle Frank teases her for being fussy by calling her a name only she knows the meaning of.

"*Siiikaaa . . .*"

After leaving the food in the kitchen I go right past them into Mimi's room. She has blossomed into the real name I never knew she had—Carmen—and has become the precious girl of the house, and my uncle and Iris will do almost anything for her. On her bed are at least fifty pretty and perfect dolls. Right now she's dressing to meet her boyfriend, Manny, slipping more and more white petticoats on over her head. Her friends from upstairs, sisters Divina, Blanca, and Lucy, perfume the room. Lucy is pale white with black hair and her red lips pop.

"Let me have some of that red lipstick," says Divina, who is ginger-colored with freckles.

"No," says Lucy. "You look better in coral lipstick."

"Baloney, she looks better in like a burgundy color," says Blanca.

They giggle and their petticoats float all over, and I wonder how Blanca's parents knew to name her "White." What if she had turned out dark?

"I wonder who is going to be at the party."

They all turn to Lucy, who has dared to bring up what is on everybody's mind—a party.

"Well, Manny is taking me. He wouldn't let me go alone," Carmen answers proudly, playing a 45 record on her little pink portable player.

The girls' sudden squealing drowns out the song's beginning, and then, just as suddenly, they bow their heads and somberly sing along like it's a church hymn. Their faces glow with hotness and little shiny beads of sweat pop up, decorating their upper lips as they move and press their shins against the bed frame, grinding with imaginary boys just out of their reach.

They sing out the last line of the song and aren't even embarrassed about singing and all that goes with it. After the song plays, Carmen finishes teasing her hair and smoothing out just the top of it, then hardening the whole thing in place with hair spray. Then she leads them, like a line of princesses, out of the apartment.

"*Bendición. Adiós,*" they all sing out.

The TV, with Mickey resting his head on Chaty's thigh, still mesmerizes the boys, and my uncle and Iris have made up. She is making coffee for him as he listens to a baseball game on two radios set to two different stations in order to not miss a thing.

Outside the girls fill the stoop with their dresses. They are quiet as they look up and down the street. Suddenly a small man appears. My cousin's friends tense up. As he gets closer I see that he has very fierce blue eyes in his bony head.

"*Bendición, Papá . . .*" says Lucy nervously.

"What are you all doing out here?" he threatens hotly.

"There's a little party," offers Divina weakly.

"A little party?" He gasps as if he's never heard of a "party" in his life.

"It's just for a little while," adds Blanca.

"Get upstairs! All of you!"

And in a microsecond three skirts switch in an about-face and scurry into the building like birds that suddenly take flight. I stare at Carmen.

"He never lets them go anywhere," she says.

"But they were all dressed up."

"They think if he sees them all dressed up he'll feel sorry for them and let them go . . . but he never does."

"Oh . . ."

Carmen looks up and down the street again and spies a dark man with sinewy arms. It's her boyfriend, Manny, and I love his Indian look. They kiss when he reaches her and their eyes shut down to dreamy, his chest just touching her breasts, both of them forgetting I am there.

"Bye," I say, turning home toward Third Avenue.

They smile, heading in the opposite direction, and I can't wait to be a teenager like they are even if it means having bigger breasts than I have now. After a while the whole family is in love with their love affair and always sigh and smile when they say, "Carmen and Manny this . . ." and "Carman and Manny that . . ."

But Carmen is always fainting and nobody knows why—it seems the more they date the more she faints and the doctors can never find anything wrong with her. The family becomes more and more grateful that Manny is always there to catch her—as a matter of fact, Manny is always there! On Saturday mornings he accompanies Iris to the supermarket so he can carry her groceries, and on Saturday nights she convinces him to chaperone Uncle Frank to keep him out of bars!

"Just tell her we have to go see about a job . . ." my uncle begs, suggesting an alternate plan.

"But, Frank," says Manny. "I don't want to lie to your wife . . ."

"It's not a lie . . . we *will* go see about a job . . . we'll just have a few drinks on the way . . ."

Manny is with them so much I'm surprised he has time for Carmen at all. But he does, and I hope I become the precious girl of the house someday like Carmen and get a boyfriend like Manny so the whole family sighs and swoons when they think of *us*.

Carmen is sixteen and they decide to get married when she finishes high school. My uncle insists Manny propose and give her the ring publicly, at a family party. The apartment on Fulton Avenue is full of relatives on Iris's side of the family, seldom seen by me. I imagine dating Iris's two beautiful nephews Gilbert and Nelson—Gilbert is white and Nelson is Indian-looking. If I got engaged to them would they hold me tight and grind against me like Carmen's friends grind their shins against the bed frame?

Everyone is dressed up—even Chaty and Mickey. Chaty has grown up into his real name, Reynaldo, which I never even knew he had. And though Mickey's real name is Francisco, we continue to call him Mickey because of his brain trouble. The girls wear lots of petticoats under their skirts and the guys wear tight pants that just touch their ankles. They dance to the Platters and Richie Ray. But Carmen's friends from upstairs, Lucy, Divina, and Blanca, are not there because even though Lucy is not married or even engaged she has gotten pregnant. I hear whispers in the kitchen.

"What happened?" asks Ma.

"Le hicieron el daño," replies Iris.

She was "wronged," and I ask Ma what that means.

"It means she is having a baby even though she is not married."

"But how could that happen? I thought God sent babies after people got married?"

"Shhh!"

"But didn't He know she wasn't married yet?"

Suddenly a commotion in the living room draws us into a sea of slim legs and petticoats parting, making way for Carmen and Manny. He ends up against the wall, all nervous and sweaty, my uncle standing over him, Carmen shyly holding his hand. In a soft voice Manny asks Carmen to marry him. We all strain to hear her whispery "yes." Then Uncle Frank takes the stage.

"I am so happy for my daughter. But I must say to Manny in front of all our friends and neighbors . . ."

"Sí, señor . . ." says Manny.

"If you ever lay a hand on her I will have to break your fucking face."

Everyone is quiet as Manny gulps and answers, *"Sí, señor."*

Manny becomes part of the family.

Soon after, God makes another mistake and sends Little Eddie's sister, Zoraida, a baby as well.

"Bless me, Father, for I have sinned. It has been one week since my last confession," I confess on Saturday so I can eat the body and blood of Christ on Sunday.

"What are your sins?" I am asked.

But he doesn't sound like Father Fitzgerald, the priest who usually hears my sins. Then I remember. Father Fitzgerald ran off with one of the Daughters of Mary—they were a group of young ladies who sang and performed special services for the church. I confess my regular series of sins.

"I disobeyed my mother, I ate bacon on Friday . . ."

"Anything else?" asks this new priest.

". . . I cursed my father in my head."

"Anything else?"

"I danced around in my panties."

There is a pause and I decide to confess something new—the sins caused by my erupting body.

"I touched myself."

The Father is quiet, then he asks, "How?"

I'm shocked. Father Fitzgerald never asked for details. I don't answer.

"Well?" he presses.

Shouldn't he know? I think. I still don't answer. It's too private— besides, if God knows everything shouldn't He know *this*?

"Were you alone?"

I feel uncomfortable and make something up. But he presses.

"Was anybody watching?"

I don't say anything.

"Well?" he asks.

"No," I say.

I hear his sigh, disgusted with my silence, as he gives me a bunch of Our Fathers and Hail Marys to recite. I don't care, I won't talk about my body with him even as it betrays me with feet growing at an alarming rate and Ma giving me dirty looks because new shoes are needed to relieve cramped toes, and now we have to shop for a training bra because my breasts are even more troublesome than my feet.

I never go to confession again.

One Saturday a group of girls I never saw before wander onto our block on their way someplace else and stop to play a game. Black girls are the best Double Dutch jumpers, with their fast counting and the sexy, tough swaying of the hips they do. This is not the very first time I have jumped Double Dutch, so I do well enough to be allowed to play awhile, and we all begin to take turns as naturally as if we had been playing together for years. Before I know it, I am in the Double Dutch zone and can almost totally keep up with them, when I feel neighborhood man-eyes looking at my chest. I am wearing a blue blouse that has two rickrack openings down the front from shoulder to hip. I don't know where my training bra has gone and I know that skin is showing through the shirt's rickrack decoration. The men are as interested in the two bumps growing on my chest as the train passenger, the parks department worker, and the pharmacist had been.

I call for a time-out and leave the girls so I can run upstairs and try to do something about this situation. But when I get inside my mother is too distracted, too busy doing laundry, and too busy talking to Uncle Eddie to help me.

I can't wait for her to finish gossiping so I frantically peek out the window to see if the girls are still there, and they are, but they won't wait forever. I have to come up with a solution quick. Aha! The answer comes to me in a flash—toilet tissue! Pinning two strips of paper with straight pins to the inside of my shirt, I manage to cover the openings. Then, I run back downstairs, almost bumping into my mother's other brother, Uncle Frank, who is on his way upstairs.

"Bendición."

"Dios te bendiga."

Blessed, I rejoin the game. But trying to play as hard as the black girls do only makes the straight pins prick me. Still, I jump and get almost as good as they are at this game (for a Puerto Rican anyway) when I see my father coming up the street.

I check out his mood as quickly as I can and am relieved that he doesn't look drunk . . . but I can see that he looks sterner and sterner the closer he gets.

"Ven acá . . ." I stop jumping. Whack! Whack! The ropes hit the sides of my legs. It hurts but I don't let on as I step over the ropes to find out what Pops wants. He stares at me like I am supposed to know what he is thinking, but I can't read his mind no matter how hard I try.

"Why are you shaking your hips to attract men?" he demands.

For a few sickening moments, I review my actions in the last half hour to see if I had somehow been doing what he says, but no— when all my marbles roll back into their proper places in my head I know that I hadn't been trying to attract men. Still—there is no answer but to stand there and wish the ground would swallow me up. In the time it took me to walk away from the game and be accused by my father, the girls wound up their rope and took off.

My father turns to go upstairs and I am left with no choice but to follow. Sour and hollow, I ignore the grown-up talk and mope around the living room until I hear the word *pregnant*.

I go into the kitchen.

Uncle Frank barks, "Here we are starving to death and you women keep having babies."

My mother turns away as if she's been slapped, and I almost fall down. I have always understood that someday we are going to run away and live happily ever after without my father. How are we going to do that if she keeps having babies?

Petey is born around the time that Aurea is eighteen years old and making plans to move to California.

"But why so far, Aurea?" Ma cries.

I know why.

Ma names the new baby Enrique. Aurea nicknames him Petey and escapes west.

I miss Aurea all the summers I have to take care of Joe as Petey goes to a neighbor for care. A routine sets in with Joe and me. We sleep in as long as possible, we eat the lumpy oatmeal Ma leaves for us, I look through the *TV Guide* to see if there are any movie musicals to watch; after the movie I make tuna-fish sandwiches, fill a thermos with Kool-Aid, and drag Joe to the park.

On Fulton Avenue we find Little Eddie and the Fulton cousins. I sit in the metal bucket seat of a swing while Little Eddie twists the whole thing around until the chains groan—then hangs on as the swing unravels (and our brains along with it). Sometimes we all sit on a seesaw and bang each end into the ground as hard as possible to knock one another off.

When we are tired of that I spread the blanket, watch the ants get into the tuna, hope nobody kicks over the Kool-Aid. It's only 11:30 a.m. when we are done. We don't know what else to do. The time we kill before Ma gets home, kills us.

CHAPTER 12

Knives in the Oven

But one night the following summer, after the day has dragged itself into darkness, I find myself alone. Where is everybody? Then I remember Ma went to pick Aurea up at the airport! She's coming back from California. At the window I look at planes in the sky and wonder which one is hers. Waiting, I listen for any noise of people at the door, but all I hear is the tired building groaning as it readjusts itself, muted voices from other apartments, radiators echoing, and mice scurrying in the wall. Time stretches longer and longer and even the train seems late in coming. In the space of waiting and sitting I am an easy target for all the creepy thoughts and bad imaginings flying around the air, like sharp shards of glass in space. Willing these bad thoughts away before they form takes all my energy. What is it that I don't want to think? The thought comes through of my father, drunk, and then what? I don't know, or do I? So I push the thought away as I nonchalantly hide the knives in the oven as if someone else were doing it, and pray for a grown-up to arrive.

I even wish that my uncle Frank and the cousins would come bursting through the door. I used to love their unexpected visits, but I'm ten years old, not a kid anymore, and now I don't like it when they barge in and make noise interrupting whatever I was doing or whatever I was watching on television; but at this moment I want them to appear. If they just walked in this very minute I promise God I won't mind if they interrupt the last five minutes of *Walt Disney's Wonderful World of Color* for the rest of my life. If they just walked in in the next five minutes I wouldn't care if Mickey wrestled Reynaldo to the floor and farted on his head. But they don't come in and I run out of things to promise God. So I decide to call them so they'll take the hint and come on over. Or maybe even invite me over to their house. I can be there in minutes. Iris answers.

"*Es Sonia . . .*"

"*¿Qué pasa . . . ?*"

"*Mami no está . . .*" But after I tell her that Ma isn't home—that she went to the airport—I don't know what to say next.

"Aha," says Iris.

"*Papi no está . . .*" She must know what I mean when I say that "my father is not home," but there is only a long silence, then a cough. Again, I tell her that my father isn't home yet—surely this will make clear to her what is not clear to me.

"Somebody will come home soon," she says so quietly I can barely hear her.

"Wait," I say.

"Really, they will." She hangs up. I listen to the empty sound that connects us before hanging up. The train swooshes by outside but I don't want a train—I want the plane my sister is supposed to be on to have landed a while ago, and for Ma and Aurea to be at the door now, now, now, now! Why won't they come home? My heart beats like I've been running though I am only standing still on alert . . . !

Suddenly there is a noise at the door. And when I hear my mother and sister enter, I run toward them and collapse in Ma's arms, giggling, relieved, and feeling foolish.

"What's the matter? *AveMaríaPurísima,* you should be hugging your sister, not me."

I hug my sister and let their arrival wash away the stupid, bad, impossible things I had imagined. Ma makes coffee and we eat cake and Aurea talks about California and then my father comes home and grunts and sits and plays his guitar and I can't even remember what I had been so scared of—so stupid of me to make things up.

Aurea gets an apartment in Queens that she shares with a roommate. Ma and I visit them in their clean space. I wear my hair in curlers and clutch my purse under my arm, looking like Aunt Iris when she visits us. The apartment has light-colored furniture called Danish. Aurea sleeps on the pullout couch.

She introduces us to her chubby roommate.

Ma looks around sadly. "If this is what you want . . ."

Aurea looks at me. "Stay over," she says.

"I . . ."

"I'll take her back tomorrow." And Ma, outnumbered, says "okay" and leaves.

I sleep with my sister on the pullout couch, and when we awaken, the day is raining and gloomy.

The chubby roommate showers and wraps herself up in a fluffy robe.

I smell bacon, eggs, toast, coffee, and orange juice. Then, with curlers still in her hair, Chubby sets out a nice place mat with a napkin and a knife and fork for herself. Then she serves herself her nice breakfast and begins to eat.

After Chubby eats she retreats to her room and reappears in full makeup and her Eastern Airlines uniform. She has taken out her rollers but not combed out her fat yellow curls. Instead, she wraps her head and neck loosely with a scarf, just like Katharine Hepburn in the movies.

"How come you don't comb your hair out?" I ask.

"I will at the office. I don't want my curls to be ruined by the damp weather."

On my way back to the Bronx with Aurea I think of how my mother is always racing out of the house to work with us hanging all over her before dropping us off to wherever we have to be for the day. I think of how Ma always feeds us first with a "hurry up and be done with it" look so she can finally eat, always last and standing at the stove. And if it's raining she sure doesn't have a nice-fitting raincoat and matching umbrella like Chubby does.

On the day I notice an A&P supermarket is going up across the street our usual routine goes slightly off. There is nothing on the television worth watching. Ma has left pancake batter for breakfast. I pour the batter in a hot skillet and yell for Joe. No answer. "Joe! Where are you? Come and get breakfast!" I run around the apartment but can't find him. Finally I look out of the window and see him out on the fire escape.

"Joe, get in here . . . the pancake is going to burn!" He leans away from me. I run back into the kitchen to check on breakfast and discover that the batter has spread right up to the sides of the pan, making the pancake hard to flip, so I dig in with the spatula and flip it onto itself like it's scrambled eggs, then run back to the window to get Joe.

"Joe! Get in here!"

He gives me a dirty look and tries to run up the fire escape steps, but I grab him by the neck and watch him slip through the opening of the fire escape in one long second—but he manages to hook his arms and legs on the sides. That stops us both. We stare at each other in hatred; I smell the pancake burning, pull him into the apartment, rush into the kitchen, toss the pancake mess onto a plate, and slam it on the table. He slinks in. "Eat it!" I command. Right after breakfast, I make the tuna-fish sandwich and Kool-Aid lunch to have in the park. I pack a blanket and some Superman comics.

Joe and I are wandering around the playground after lunch and the whole day is yawning in front of us when suddenly I see my mother frantically signaling to us. What is she doing home so early? But before that can register, I see my father stumbling toward her. I grab the thermos and blanket and approach my parents. I smell a new danger. As I get closer, I can hear him saying bad things about her. She grabs Joe and the thermos from me when I reach them— and we start for home. She walks slow and steady and all I can think of is Christ carrying His cross. My father walks all crazy, sometimes quick and sometimes slow and sloppy, darting in front and in back of her. I stick close to her, hanging on and looking for some kind of explanation. But her face is set, grim.

People walk along with us before they know they are in the middle of a fight. I look to the strangers for some sort of explanation, but none comes. After the passersby see what they have stepped into, they carefully step back and stand to watch as if we are a parade.

Some curious ones follow at a distance. I do both. First, I walk along with my parents for a while, and then I join the ones following, trying to look like I'm just a curious person, too, and don't really know those three people jerking around in front of me. Neither of my parents notices me playing this game of being both part of them and not.

We turn the corner and walk past Don Joe's bodega. He comes out, wiping his massive hands on his bloodstained apron, and slowly shaking his head, watches us enter our building. We continue up the stairs, slow and steady.

I am bringing up the rear and see Genoveva open her door, then close it partway, leaving it open enough to peek out at us as if she is hungry. Half-dressed Flor comes out to see the action, La Puerca/Bizca opens her door and I wish I could yell that she's stinking up the hallway with the smell from her messy apartment. All the Cabezas stick their heads out their door.

My mother passes them silently as if she is a queen and they are a bunch of nobodies. She keeps one landing's space between her and my father, who is tripping up the stairs. And then, at a certain moment, when she is right above him and all eyes are on her, she does the unthinkable—she swings the thermos up in the air and bashes it down onto his head with such force the thermos breaks open.

The neighbors gasp as tiny, clean, white pieces of granular foam insulation swirl all around, turning the dark and dirty stairwell into a place of snowy beauty. The world goes into slow motion, the particles land on my head, my shoulders, and eyelashes, and my heart swells with joy and pride.

———

Months later I'm running down the stairs from my apartment, flying high on the announcement that we are moving.

"It's that damned bodega," offers Genoveva. "Now, he won't have such an easy place to drink in."

"A bigger apartment will be real nice," offers Doña Cabeza.

"Remember, you work," says Flor enviously.

I am sure that starting out in a new neighborhood will fix everything and that we will live happily ever after. Anything is possible.

PART 2
La Lucha

CHAPTER 1

Landing on Planet X

Where are we? What is this place? We materialize in the middle of a maze of buildings that are only six stories high—too low to be projects. The entrances to the buildings do not face a sidewalk. My parents stare at the address on a piece of paper as if they'd never seen it before, as if they'd even forgotten what paper is. I see building numbers but they are written on the sides of the structures and not above the entrance doors like they are supposed to be!

We finally find our way past a patch of grass and up a little walk that turns in on itself. Once in the apartment I run to the windows, but they face more buildings just like ours, with little lawns separating them. Where's the street? Which is the way out? Or the front and back? I cannot see who else lives around here, who is coming or going, or playing, fighting, or drinking. How will I judge my father's mood if I can't see him walking or swaying up the street?

Later, Ma stands lost in the emptiness of the living room full of boxes. My baby brother, Petey, crawls around the floor crying, and my brother Joe, in his too-tight clothes, gently pushes his tin toy car along a wall.

"*Dejen eso.*" Ma pleads with both of them to stop. Petey cannot but Joe sits still; and because he has become good at fading away we soon forget he is there. My father runs his finger along my mother's face from her ear to her cheek slowly to make her feel better but it is not enough and she turns away.

They tiptoe around, picking things up and putting them down in the same place, to avoid each other's eyes. I thought we were going to be happy moving away from the bodega and up in the world in a better neighborhood and apartment and all that, but they look sadder than ever. Not like they had made anything better, but like they had just bumped into a glass wall they hadn't seen right in front of them.

I look around. The rooms are white with no cracks to get lost or find shapes in. The floors are shiny wood, not covered in rose-patterned linoleum, and the lights built into the ceiling are fluorescent bright so we scurry around like roaches exposed by light and desperate for someplace to hide. For days we unpack slowly and I find the ceramic tropical fish I had given Ma one Mother's Day.

"Where should I put this . . . ?"

She turns to me, pained by my question. "How should I know where anything goes?" she says.

One day, after we'd been there awhile, there is a knock on the door.

"Who?" my ma fearfully asks.

"You people have to be quiet," says a pale, thin white man who lives downstairs. "My wife just had a baby and you people have to be quiet."

What's this? How can we be making any noise with my parents skimming around each other like ghosts? Even their fighting has taken on a raspy despair.

"It's no use," I hear my mother say over and over again.

"Yes, it is . . ." my father always responds.

We are all like spirits. Petey cries quietly, monotonously, I become sleepy—the whole family matches Joe in his silence. And in this ghostlike state I float to my new school.

"Cuidado," Ma shrieks as I walk out the door. "Watch where you are going! Are you sleepwalking or something?" But her words just bounce off me. I am not awake enough for her to get through to me. I have gotten good at walking, talking, and even eating while being half-awake. After weeks of floating out the front door of my building, then turning left to go right, around the scraggly playground, only to sometimes find myself back where I have started, I have finally figured the way out of the maze and am able to reach my goal—the street from which I see the overpass that will take me to school. There is no beautiful elevated train in this neighborhood, only the traffic of Bruckner Boulevard. Once on the overpass I look down on the traffic, always a *tapón*, clogged with cars barely moving.

In school I go along with the herd of kids shifting left and right as they go in and out of classes. If I stay quiet I can feel the movement of the group and go along without thinking. I always find myself between two Spanish girls, Norma and Teresa. Are they my new friends? I don't know. In class I stare out the window.

"Sonia."

It's the teacher, Miss Pellman, pulling me back into the classroom. "Would you like to clean the erasers?"

I replay her words in my mind. If I say no she'll ask me, "Why not?" Saying yes and then doing it will mean less talking. So I say yes. When I'm finished with the job I get lost picking at a scab.

"Sonia?"

It's Miss Pellman again.

"Can you hand out the notebooks?"

Why does she keep waking me up? Why won't she leave me alone? I hand out the notebooks and a girl trips me and I wonder if I will get another scab to play with where my knee has scraped the floor. Norma (or Teresa) helps me up. When I go to the bathroom Miss Pellman sends Norma or Teresa with me. When we must draw pictures for Pan-American Week, I draw with Norma or Teresa. Norma is white with thick, straight, brown hair and one eyebrow that goes across her forehead. She wears gym socks and Buster Brown shoes. Teresa has skin more like mine, and frizzy hair that has to be controlled with a headband. She has dark circles under her eyes and finely wrinkled thick lips. We cross the overpass on our way home, then go our separate ways because this neighborhood is fake and spread out and unnatural. If it was natural my school friends would be my neighborhood friends. When Teresa, Norma, and I part, I walk a ways with a Negro girl.

I'm not really with her and she is not really with me but I notice that of all the kids in the school she lives a bit closer to me. One day the hollow feeling in me is so great I talk to her.

"You know I live right over there . . ."

She tries to figure me out but says nothing.

"Do you want to come and play . . . ?"

She says yes and suddenly I'm shy.

Ma is annoyed when Rhonda comes to the door. Not because she is black, I don't think, but because there is no time for friendships and hanging out in my house when, despite the boredom, we live like there could be an explosion any minute. Rhonda and I go into my room and she looks around and I wonder if she thinks it odd that there's hardly any furniture, so I decide to act like the lack of furniture is new to me, too, as I set up a board game. It's called Girlfriends and played by blonde and red-haired girls on television commercials. The fluorescent light makes Rhonda's black skin bluish and my brown skin gray—not at all like the creamy pink girls we are trying to be.

Before the first round is over I begin to feel sleepy and she starts to forget when it's her turn. "I kind of have to go soon," she says after a while. The sky gets purple and it is time for my father to come home and Ma hides the knives in the oven and signals to me that Rhonda must go, because you never know what can happen. Rhonda and I hardly look at each other when we say good-bye at the door, then I go back to my room and fall asleep as fast and hard as I can.

The next morning I dress and start out the door when Ma pulls me back into the apartment. She holds up my pajamas, which have a brownish-red stain on them, as evidence of a crime committed. Ma pushes me into the bathroom, pulls down my panties, and makes me step into a ring of elastic with two fasteners, front and back. I know what this is—I've seen it in the bathroom over the years, sometimes drying on the curtain rod like a weak little snake, and sometimes hidden in big box of Kotex behind and under the sink. Grimly attaching a sanitary napkin to the two fasteners and making sure it's snug between my legs she sends me on my way. I feel like I am wearing a mustard plaster. But mustard plasters are on your chest when you're sick and can't breathe. Am I sick down there?

It hits me when I see Teresa and Norma on the overpass. I have gotten my period. *¡Me cantó el gallo!* The rooster has sung to me. That's how my aunts Bon Bon and Iris talked about it. When somebody got their period they said the rooster sang to them. Even in New York? I'm so happy that anything has happened to me.

"I got my period," I crow to Norma and Teresa as soon as I see them. Why is the expression that the "rooster sang to me," when *I'm* the one who is crowing all loud and tough and special? No one is singing to me, I am singing to myself.

"Wow," says Norma.

"Did you get yours yet?" I ask.

"No."

"How about you, Teresa?"

"No," she confesses like the little girl she is. They both look at me like I might have a disease they don't want to catch, but I know they *do* want to catch it and be grown-up at last.

At school Miss Pellman knows right away. How does she know everything without me saying? She pats my cheek with her cool, soft hand, squeezes my shoulder, and smiles. The bathroom rules are different that day. Come 10:00 a.m. Teresa and I raise our hands. Miss Pellman gives us the okay to go, then adds, "Why don't you go along, too, Norma?" The three of us being allowed to go to the bathroom at the same time makes us expand with greatness as we float out the door. Then we are allowed the same bathroom privileges at 11:30 a.m.! The class mutters disapproval, but who cares; my period makes my two friends and me special. I am the queen and they are my ladies-in-waiting. But it only lasts for a few days and after a few months of bloody visits my troubles really begin.

CHAPTER 2

Estupida

I am in line to go outside and play at recess. Someone knocks into me and as I sprawl and look up I see the boy who has crashed into me is just as surprised as I am, but right behind him is the angry girl Denise who is always around when I fall. She has pushed him into me. Denise is black but her skin is much lighter than mine and she has a few freckles across her nose. Her hair is divided in many sections with barrettes of all colors.

"Don't look at *me*," she says, even though there is no one else to look at. My tears push forth but I open my eyes wide to accommodate them so they don't spill out.

Denise finds me no matter where I am. Even when *I* don't know where I am. Every day she pushes, or pinches, or shoves. Norma and Teresa know and they look on, all wide-eyed and feeling sorry for me, but I think they like the show. I never see Denise's punches or pinches coming, but even if I did I wouldn't fight back. For weeks I just crawl into myself like a poked crab.

One day Norma warns me, "Oh, you are going to get it today . . ."

"What?"

"Denise said she was going to fight you today, after gym."

All the other kids must've known, too, because after gym, silently in the hallway, my classmates form a circle in which to see the spectacle. Denise moves toward the center of the empty space they make, and everyone, including Teresa and Norma, pulls away from me so I am isolated. All energy drains from me and flows into the floor that I wish would absorb me. I'm scared for my face, my ears, my legs, my chest, and I wish I could put myself in my own pocket and become lint. Denise takes aim and when I think I will be pulverized Miss Pellman appears like a fairy godmother in a Grimm fairy tale! She waves us back into an orderly line and my classmates transform back into little girls and boys and not bloodthirsty fighters and spectators.

"You're lucky," whispers Norma.

"She never comes this way," adds Teresa.

"How would you like to be in a spelling bee?" Miss Pellman asks, as if I just hadn't been so close to losing my life. I try to focus on her. She is always comfortable, clean, and neat in her thin wool sweaters and skinny belts and suede shoes. Her hair is so nice and brown, held back off her face with a headband. I think her legs are so pretty but *she* is not, really, because her nose is too long and thin. I can't think of anything to say, though I know I don't want to be in a contest.

"Don't worry, you just do the best you can, and it'll be all right."

Later, I look at all the words I am supposed to know and am surprised at the way *cocoa* is spelled with an "a" at the end. It makes no sense. You can't hear that "a" at the end of the word. Up on the stage in the auditorium on the day of the spelling bee I am nervous and hope I am good enough for Miss Pellman so she doesn't feel sorry she picked me. My turn comes! I'm asked to spell *cocoa*. Oh no, it's that tricky word with the "a" at the end! Maybe I studied it wrong. I can't be sure of what I know. Maybe I saw an "a" that wasn't there?

"Cocoa, c-o-c-o, cocoa," I spell.

I am disqualified immediately and later when I have to face Miss Pellman I feel ashamed.

"Oh, don't worry about it," she says impatiently.

Later at recess I stand by the fence thinking about how stupid I am and wonder why I had been afraid to spell *cocoa* correctly, when suddenly a ball bounces off my head. Who threw it?

"Ha-ha!" A big, fat boy with white hair and eyebrows and yellow teeth comes toward me.

"Sorry," he giggles, looking to retrieve his ball.

I hold the sore spot on my head and when I catch sight of his soft, white, marshmallow neck, a white-hot fury comes over me and makes me jump on his back and bite. I am yanked into the principal's office.

"People eat! People chew!" the principal screams. "Only animals bite! Are you an animal?"

Then he calls my mother at the factory. When she gets home that night she is furious because she has to take off from work to come into school. We need the money. How can I be so thoughtless? Am I crazy—making the teacher notice me like that!

A few days later she comes to school, but there is something else on her mind. She half listens to the principal's complaints about me. Driving home I look at her and it's like she is making the car move with her own energy, not gas or wheels. Her eyes bug out and her hair is flying back out of the way. We get home and I'm surprised to see Bon Bon packing old suitcases with our clothes. I'm told to pack as well.

"Pack? Why?"

"Why do you think? We are moving now, quickly, before your father comes home!"

How crazy is that? Nothing had happened. No big fight. Just avoided glances and heaviness in the air.

"*¡Avanza!*" my mother yells and I hurry as best I can. But move what? The refrigerator? The stove? I push it.

"*¡Muchacha!*" She can't believe how stupid I am. "Put your clothes in this bag!" I wish I could get in the bag *myself* and throw myself out the window and fall into the maze, where it would take weeks to find me. But we put ourselves in the car and drive to an apartment on Washington Avenue, right near where we used to live on Third Avenue. The building is old and rickety and breaking down, the wooden door frame soft. Inside Joe is fascinated that his toys roll and gather in one corner because the floor has such an angle in it, and though the apartment is tiny—three furnished rooms and a kitchen—Ma gets lost in it. Joe tries to dress himself and puts his right shoe on his left and vice versa. Petey weeps.

I wonder what my father will think when he comes home and finds us gone. Will he peer around shocked and bewildered, not knowing where to look? My mother is gazing around, surprised and bewildered in this new apartment even though moving was her idea. We settle, not into the apartment but more like into ourselves, each of us separately.

Then a surprise! A day later Bon Bon shows up with my cousin Zoraida, who now has a brand-new teen name—Sue. With a toddler in tow and a baby in the oven she doesn't have a place to stay. Bon Bon helps her daughter move in—Ma looks like she got hit in the head with a baseball bat.

"She'll take care of Joe and Petey when you work," Bon Bon assures her.

Is this good or bad? I look to my mother for how to feel, but I can't understand her face so I look to Sue. I like Sue. She reminds me of the beautiful actress Kim Novak, tall and with a nice straight nose. Bon Bon gets ready to leave but waits until her little grandson is not looking to suddenly smack him on the legs. Hard. He turns to her, his face contorted, uncomprehending, tears welling up and spilling out all over the place. I stare at Bon Bon.

"To ward off the evil eye," she says.

That night Ma and Sue put the chairs facing each other to make a bed for the little boy and pregnant Sue sleeps on the sofa.

I share the back room with Joe, and Petey sleeps with Ma. I look out the window. The Fenway movie theater Aurea and I used to go to is across our street, and watching its lights blinking on and off in big, red, neon letters I think I'm not the only stupid one in this bunch.

CHAPTER 3

West Side Story

Though we've moved it's decided that I finish out the school year in Miss Pellman's class. It takes a long time to get there even with Ma dropping me off at a convenient bus stop on her way to work. "Just until the school year runs out," Ma hisses at me. "Then you'll go to a school around here." I half listen, or not at all, to anyone, not even Miss Pellman when she greets me each morning.

"Sonia . . ."

Miss Pellman's lips are moving. *Nice color lipstick*, I think.

"On Saturday . . . can you come?"

I wonder how come she is not married. And I think that's a real good way to be—not married—free to be whatever you want to be—

"I can talk to your mother if you want to."

But do I want to be an old maid like Miss Pellman, a *jamona* . . . ?

"I would like to take you, Norma, and Teresa . . ."

Being an old maid would not be bad if I had a job . . .

"Sonia!"

I snap out of it. "What?"

"I would like to take you, Norma, and Teresa to see *West Side Story* on Saturday. Would you like that?"

"*West Side Story*?"

"It's a movie. Made from a musical."

My father is not around to automatically say no to me about doing anything that's fun so the next Saturday we are in Manhattan. Not Grandmother's El Barrio Manhattan but a Manhattan street full of movie theaters, and they are not like the small, shabby Fenway theater, either, but have big marquees with blinking lights that work. Inside there are tons of excited people and large posters of movie stars everyplace I look. Finding our seats we settle, with Miss Pellman sitting on one side of me and Teresa and Norma sitting on the other. Folks are chewing popcorn and chattering all around but when the movie starts silence falls on the spectators like a blanket from above. The sudden quiet stirs me and I look up from my lap to the screen.

I see the schoolyards, the fences, the buildings, and candy stores I've seen in all my neighborhoods—but here they look different. Sharp, clear, bright, and beautiful. What is this that I am watching?

There is something different about the familiar indoor scenes as well. But here a guitar leaning against the wall looks romantic. The shadows of holy crosses on the homemade altars are so mysterious I quickly give religion a second thought—and seeing an actress wearing a cross daintily on her chest nails it for me. I, too, want to wear a sexy cross between my breasts. The colors I see are hot pink and turquoise and purple, but they are bold and important and meaningful, not just loud. I stare at the screen with some mental distance so I can reason and figure it out but there is no figuring to do, because when the actors sing and dance on a roof about being in America my heart takes over and begins to beat faster and faster until it makes a racket in my ears that roars.

My soul or some power inside me begins to rise and I panic—will there be enough room in my body for this new feeling? *Make way, make way,* a voice inside me shouts. I sit up taller, because if I don't accommodate this emotion it will spill out and explode, maybe even hurting those around me. My eyes open wider so I can see everything better. My ears pick up all the musical sounds flowing and crashing into each other in the air, and I wonder, how long have I been sleeping? My God, how long have I been unconscious and missing everything all around me? Asleep! Asleep! Asleep. Like a drugged person, like Dennis the junkie nodding out on Third Avenue. Is Ma right? Am I always daydreaming? Asleep, yes, but daydreaming, no . . . not really. Daydreams are possibilities. I never daydream anything I think could actually happen. I didn't know what things were possible.

This movie makes things possible. Music and words and songs and images that are possible. *Breathe,* I tell myself, *breathe before you explode and somehow miss the end of this scene, or the end of this song, calm down, calm down until the end of this movie.* And I almost make it but don't because finally I cannot control any longer this thing that must come out—but wait—it's not "this thing" at all. There's nothing "inside me" coming out, like something I ate and shouldn't have—it's the "me" myself that is coming out. The "me" that will not be afraid to see and feel and hear whatever gets in my way.

Shedding my old, sleepy cocoon so the real me can rise makes me giggle, and then laugh, but too soon the new me, the one who feels the air around and is being born too fast, begins to cry—no, not cry, but sob, gasp, and gush. I am all tears and choking breath and loud noise, and all this honking makes people in the theater look at me, and I look back and see the red curtain closing over the screen and excited people reach for their coats and jackets and finally I see that

Miss Pellman is alarmed, and I struggle to suck it up when I see that Teresa has seen me crying and is trying to cry, too! But it's fake, fake crying.

No, no, no, I think. This sadness is mine. All mine. This sorrow at how stupid people hurt each other in the movies and in real life is mine, all mine, and dumb Teresa cannot have any of my despair.

Miss Pellman whisks me to the bathroom and pats my face with cold water.

"Calm down, calm down," she says.

I don't want to calm down. "Calm down" means lie down and drop dead to me, and I am not going to do it. I have done enough of that. If this movie can happen, what else? Women and girls come into the bathroom and pee and flush the toilet and wash their hands near us and Miss Pellman smiles at them weakly and says, "She's all right, a little overcome by the movie, is all . . ."

It's more—and not only *that*—I don't care that strangers see me cry. These tears are important and I will not hold anything back at all. This sadness is not the usual sluggish, lethargic, somber one I didn't even know I have gotten used to—this sadness is exhilarating, active, and relentless, like a wave that keeps knocking you down at Far Rockaway Beach every time you come up for air and you like the danger of it all.

We make our way to the lobby and find Teresa and Norma. The girls stare at me, and Miss Pellman tries to make things nice.

"Would you girls like posters?"

We all want posters but that is the only way we are alike. I am not like Teresa and Norma, I am like me; and I'll take the poster but I *won't* let it calm me down; I'm keeping this feeling of aliveness, of importance, of bigness and activity no matter what happens next.

Hanging on to the poster like it's a life raft, I let it help me get through the "good-byes" and "thank you, Miss Pellman" and all the rest as I resentfully leave Manhattan to go back to my mother and her ridiculous nose-to-ground slavishness. Clutching the poster to my heart, I make my way home through sticky tears that harden down my cheeks.

"How was the movie?" Ma asks.

I don't know what to say. This apartment is too small to hold the feelings that she will never understand, and anyway it is too full of the smell of dirty diapers for me to want to share any of the beauty that is going on inside me. I am big and important now with lots and lots of important things to do; and so I go into the only room with a door that's not the bathroom.

"*AveMaríaPurísima*," Ma mutters, giving up.

Unfolding my beautiful possession on the bed, I lie down next to it and look at the movie stars from an angle. They looked so beautiful singing and kissing on their fire escape that I have to touch their faces, and the fire escape and all that touching releases a dull, droning river of over-stored tears, different from the ones I shed in the movie theater. But when I touch the image of the old buildings that fade into white background I cry harder because they remind me of all the buildings my family have moved in and out of in the Bronx, looking for something they will never get.

My mauling does some damage to the poster but suddenly other thoughts make me ignore it altogether. I sit up in the bed, push the movie souvenir aside, get up, and look out the window. I'm alive and awake now and I think again, *If people can make that movie, what can I do?*

CHAPTER 4

Fight! Fight! Fight!

The movie made me strong. I can fight now. So I'm okay at the end of the term when I leave Miss Pellman's class to go to J.H.S. 55 on Webster Avenue where every new student gets beat up. I don't even try to avoid corners with tough-looking girls—which would've been impossible unless I went to school by way of Brooklyn—and I even walk by Brenda and her gang, Toni, Cynthia, and Martha. Toni is tall and thin with fluffy hair and says the way to not get pregnant is to wash with Pepsi-Cola after you do it. Cynthia is muscular and wears her hair in a French twist, and I think she secretly likes me but can't show it because it would be letting her friends down. Martha is very dark and tiny as a whisper. But Brenda is built like a football player. Her hair is almost too short to straighten; yet she does, so there are straight strands of hair on top, covering some other kind of hair underneath. She is so tough she threw a guy against a wall after he quipped, "Hey, Brenda, tell your mother to stop wearing lipstick, she's leaving rings around my dick." Before he could snicker even once Brenda laid him out! She has a natural mean look but one day she doesn't look so tough.

I hang out in the back of the classroom but still hear.

"Brenda, what's up?" asks Toni.

"Nothin'."

"Whatchu mean, 'nothin'?" says Toni. "Your mother's coming in, that's what's up!"

"Why don't you shut up, Toni!" Brenda barks.

"You want to make me?" Toni laughs.

"Somebody's gonna get a whuppin' tonight," giggles Martha.

Later, in homeroom, a woman bursts in and looks around wildly like she's been let out of a cage. She turns left and right, looking to be attacked or ready to do the attacking herself. This woman is big and wearing an orange-and-black cloak with jagged white stripes that makes her look even bigger. Her shiny, dark, blemish-free skin is stretched perfectly over her high cheekbones, her nose is wide and delicate, but she looks angry enough to snort. She does not have any time to fool around with anybody—like she had been very busy, suddenly interrupted, and is furious about it, and I wonder if Ma looks like that when she is interrupted at work and has to come to school because of me. This woman's eyes dart around the room and land on Brenda like bullets, diminishing Brenda so she melts, quieting down the classroom. The bell rings, signaling us to go to our first class, but we wait to see what will happen.

"Mrs. Watson," the teacher says nervously. "Thank you for coming in. Let's go down to the principal's office. Brenda?"

Brenda looks like she is walking the plank as they go out the door, teacher first, Brenda, then wild-eyed Mrs. Watson. The second they are out of sight the class erupts, following them.

"Ohhh . . . man, oh man . . . Brenda gonna get it . . . oh . . ."

But I am not interested in Brenda's possible beating. I have been arrested by Mrs. Watson's hair. It stuck two inches from her head like an inky sable crown.

"What's that hair . . . ?" I whisper out loud.

"Oh . . . that's called a 'natural,'" somebody whispers back like it's a big secret.

Brenda comes in the next day angrier than ever and in the hallway I get a painful jab from her. I turn around to find all of them—Brenda, Cynthia, Toni, and Martha—giggling.

"What's wrong?" says Toni.

"Why don't you all stop," says Cynthia.

Only Brenda gives me a dead look and I know she is holding the safety pin.

Next morning I put shorts on under my skirt so the boys can't see my panties, and braid my hair in such a way that Brenda can't grab it. I want to get ready for when she grinds me into the ground. It comes right after lunch. The minute I feel a push I push back with all my might. They all, especially Brenda, are happily surprised. We plan to meet at the schoolyard after three, where Brenda, I'm sure, will kill me, but I want to get it over with.

I hear chanting all around me: "Fight! Fight! Fight!" And I don't even wait for the uncontrollable white-hot fury to wash over me like when I jumped the boy and bit him on the neck at my old school, or when I threw the plank at Little Eddie. Ducking my head, I close my eyes and whirl around with clenched fists. My fists glance her, and as she knows enough to keep her eyes open while fighting, she quickly and easily pushes me over and sits on me. I look to my left, and see, through all the jostling legs and feet, a teacher coming. A teacher! I admit, though happy to fight, I am happier to see a teacher.

"That's enough! On your way, both of you," he says gruffly.

I feel good after my brawl. It wasn't bad at all. It was like when you jump into a pool—cold at first but after a while you get used to it. I can't wait to get home to examine my split lip, but it's not as bad as I had hoped. Ma comes home.

"Hey, Ma . . ."

"Hurry up, help me with sandwiches. Iris is coming over."

She doesn't even notice my lip and I'm surprised that it doesn't matter to me, that I like having a secret. Anyway, Ma is nervous. This is Iris's first visit to our life without my father. She and my uncle Frank have been busy with the new house they bought on Elder Avenue. Treasuring my fight secret, I straighten up the apartment a little and even figure out a way to cut the ham-and-cheese sandwiches Ma has made into four pieces so it looks like we have more food. Cousin Chaty and his mother, Iris, arrive. She has taken to wearing high heels and long-line bras all the time now and smiles tightly at the way we live without a single piece of plastic-covered furniture or a mirror from the downtown Italian furniture stores.

"Ha!" laughs my cousin, taking a tiny square of food and popping it into his mouth. "Look at this! Who is this for? Midgets? Babies! Ha! Wait, I can eat this like popcorn." He tosses the bit of sandwich in the air and catches it on the way down. I laugh along but I don't feel it, and when I see Iris give him a scolding nod I know how badly we are doing. My mother is worn-out, she can't make enough money for us—this move has been futile.

It's still light out when they leave so I go back to my place at the window and notice a cute boy unloading boxes of soda for the candy store across the street. He is beautiful with thick, wavy hair and I wonder how come I've never seen him before. But no matter, buying something at the candy store is a way to get out of the house and I run to him.

"Can I have a Mallomar?"

He gives me the chocolate marshmallow cookie. I pay and leave. Outside I eat it and try to think of something else to make him want to run away with and marry me, but nothing occurs to me except buying another Mallomar.

"Can I have another Mallomar?"

He gives it to me and I take my time opening and eating it as I leave. But he doesn't say anything—so I turn around and buy another.

This time his eyes widen as he hands me one and I stay put while eating. "Will you throw this away for me?" I say, handing him the wrapper. And then it is silent except for my chewing. When I'm done I can't think of any reason to stay, and not having any more money I run upstairs and upturn all the cushions on the sofa to find some. Digging my hands deep in the crevices I come up with more change. Sue and her children are long gone but she has left plenty of pennies behind. I run across the street and buy another Mallomar.

"You sure like Mallomars!"

He speaks!

"Yes, I do," I say and wait for him to say something else, but he doesn't.

The only thing to do is eat.

"I'd like another one."

He gives me another one and shakes his head in amazement and I grin. I've impressed him!

"I'm gonna have to get another box from downstairs pretty soon if you keep eating them."

"They are my favorite. I just can't stop. That's just how I am. I can eat them all day. You might as well call me that Mallomars girl . . . or maybe just Mallo . . . but my name is Sonia. Sonia Manzano—but I should change it to Sonia Mallomar, really."

"My name is Tony . . ."

Tony, I think—like in *West Side Story* . . . ? But before I can digest that idea my stomach cramps in such a way that I am speechless.

"What's the matter?" he says.

My gut rumbles so loudly I am sure he can hear it.

"Hey, are you okay?"

I can't answer because my insides turn into liquid and threaten to gush out with the slightest move, and I have to run home and twist and writhe on the toilet until I am spent and empty and feel that I have lost because my life is so different from *West Side Story.*

It's Saturday, the morning of my fourteenth birthday.

"Happy birthday," says Ma, handing me a box.

Inside is a green dress so ugly it makes me mad. Not only because I'd never wear such a thing, but because it reminds me I have no place to wear it to.

"Thanks, Ma . . ."

"AveMaríaPurísima . . ."

My stomach feels okay by now, but I'm still embarrassed in front of the boy, whose name I don't even want to *think* because I feel like such a jerk, so I sneak past the candy store hoping he won't see me. It's rainy and muggy as I slip on over to Bathgate Avenue to buy stockings, at the same store where I had bought the handkerchiefs for Marion Uble's birthday so long ago. And that old disappointment throbs anew and gets mixed up with this fresh disappointment of being fourteen years old today.

Still, I buy a pair of stockings for fifty cents to last me the week. By the time I get home my hair is frizzy, making me look as ugly as I feel inside. I have nothing to do but look at the Fenway marquee blinking on and off, and flip through an old magazine when—bang! There it is! Everything I've been looking for. Everything that will give me joy and happiness everlasting—a short, blonde haircut like the one on a girl in a Maytag washing machine ad.

She is thin and wearing a turquoise-blue jumper over a long-sleeved white blouse, with a big bow around her neck. Her hair is all wispy bangs around her eyes, the rest of it cut bluntly at her chin. It is pale yellow and silky.

What gets me is the look of joy on her face. She's in a series of pictures with the washer/dryer. In the first picture she is happily loading in the clothes, in another she is cheerfully pouring in the detergent, in the third she is impishly waiting for the washer to be done, in the fourth she athletically tosses the clothes into the dryer, in the fifth she pirouettes while waiting, and in the sixth she's done and stands triumphantly next to a pile of freshly laundered, exquisitely folded clothes! What a life. I want to be her so I can grin and flip my troubles away with my hair while I do the laundry if we ever get a washing machine. I hound Ma, who is in the kitchen singing *"You really got a hold on me . . ."* while making spaghetti. (Another good thing about not having my father around is that we can eat more American food.)

"I want to cut my hair."

"What?"

"Like that!" I point to the girl in the magazine. "Like that. So it looks like that."

"Your hair don't go like that!" says Ma.

"It would if I could cut it!"

She laughs. "Go put your nice dress on," she says. Then she continues singing: *"Oh yeah, you really got a hold on me!"*

"No. Why get dressed when there's no place to go. I want to cut my hair!"

Ma rolls her eyes and ignores me and I fume around the apartment until it gets dark when the doorbell rings and it's Little Eddie. As always he is grinning and cheerful and does not judge the squalor we live in like Reynaldo did because Little Eddie was never like that—and behind him is a fourteen-piece band!

He has learned to play an instrument at the Boys Club of America and has become part of a group called the Caribbean Combo, and on that gloomy day he has convinced them all to show up at our apartment! They tumble into our place with instruments banging all over and begin to set up.

I am flabbergasted and don't know what to say.

"Happy birthday, cuz." He grins.

There is laughing and joking. The trombone player cracks that the apartment is so small his trombone will smack against the walls. They play and it's like the unbelievable events in a movie, like just when you think it's curtains for someone but the cops show up, or the fairy godmother happens by, or better yet, the character in the movie realizes something that enables her to save herself like Dorothy in *The Wizard of Oz*.

As they play the apartment becomes the most glorious one in the whole building, and the building becomes the most glorious one in the Bronx, which becomes the most glorious borough in New York, and New York becomes the best city in America, and America becomes the best country in the world, and the world becomes the best planet in the solar system, and I am the center of it all.

And then, without any warning, we move back in with my father.

CHAPTER 5

Southern Boulevard

W ait until you see the room . . ." says Ma.

I roll my eyes and don't answer. We are in the vestibule of the new apartment my parents have decided to try and be happy in. A squat Mexican-looking woman with two fat braids crisscrossing her head and wearing an embroidered peasant blouse is mopping up the floor in the hallway but really she's locked into our conversation as we enter the apartment's long hall. Ma sweeps Joe, Petey, and me past a kitchen, a bathroom, and into the living room. The boys run on ahead as she points out the two bedrooms to the left and right of us.

"Petey will stay with me and your father in the big room."

I wonder when my parents made up. Did he show up at her job? Did she meet him after we went to sleep? Did they meet at Lincoln Hospital after one of Joe's attacks?

"*Qué cara* . . . What a face," she says. When I don't respond she goes on, "And you and Joe will share this room."

Great, Ma.

I ignore the room and go to the window to look out on this new neighborhood. No nice shade and shadows hit the street like on Third Avenue. The sun is bright and Southern Boulevard is exposed and split right down the middle. One side of the boulevard has buildings and people and kids playing, but the other side has garages with orange-painted storefronts and awnings to service the cars that whiz by on nearby Bruckner Boulevard.

The building we have moved into is split as well. You enter a courtyard, then go left or right and up some stairs to your apartment, and I feel just like my surroundings, split in half as well, part of my family and not.

"Nice, right?"

Sure, Ma, great.

At night the commerce across the street stops, and the empty garages with Bruckner Boulevard traffic in the background give the neighborhood an eerie glow, like there are humans on one side and futuristic beings who live in cars on the other. We settle down. Joe was diagnosed with asthma and his gasping for air and Petey's crying begin to mark the passage of time. I want out, but the farthest I can get away is at the window, which becomes, like the highest point on a sinking ship, the last resort; and I do everything there, brush my hair, paint my nails, and even eat while straining and leaning out.

I discover twenty-five-cent *True Confessions* magazines with lots of great stories about women in love who have sex before they are married. Taking my magazine out the window I read, leaning on my elbows until the sill scores my forearms. The sun provides light to read my stories during the day; the streetlight illuminates the words at night.

One day I feel eyes on me from above. I look and there is a boy with sandy hair and a sharp nose hooked over small lips. Bothered by his gaze I go back to my magazine, but I can still feel his eyes boring into the top of my head. Sighing, I close my magazine so he thinks I am done reading and was going inside anyway. But he stays in my mind, so the next day I prepare for in case we meet, by making sure the hair on the top of my head is perfect.

"Why don't you go inside and read with a real light?" he says when he sees me.

I turn around and look up. "Why don't you?" I answer.

"I can't. It's the Sabbath and I'm not even allowed to turn one on."

A woman calls to him from inside his apartment: "Whaddaya doing? Larry!"

He disappears without even saying good-bye. The next night I brush my hair at the window, one hundred strokes (just like I read in a magazine that a woman should do) so he can see how long and gorgeous it is. I begin. One stroke, two strokes, three strokes—by the time I get to fifty strokes and I haven't felt any vibrations from above I peek. He is not there and I feel like an asshole.

But often he is there and I get a sexy, flirty feeling as we talk with me on the bottom and him on the top even though there is an apartment between us. We sort of telepathically communicate to each other from our windows, and even know to ignore each other when his parents are with him in the hallway or street. It is only at our windows that we become so real to each other we can almost feel each other's breath.

One day I paint my nails Pearl White and wave my fingers around.

"Are they dry . . . ?"

He's there.

"Yes. Do you like the color?" I say, twisting around to look up.

"I can't see."

"Look." I stretch my fingers way up above my head like I want a hug.

"Nice . . . I guess . . ."

I find him funny and laugh at his remark.

"Seems like a silly thing to do, though," he says.

"What? My nails?"

"Yes."

"What about not being able to turn on a light?" I say.

"It's my religion . . ."

"Can you turn on the TV?"

"No."

"How about doing your nails then?"

He laughs at my joke and my neck is trembling with the effort but still I smile up at him, and he smiles down on me. We say nothing important and barely listen to each other's words but are in touch and as close as if we were in the same room keeping a secret so forbidden we even hide it from each other.

I'm enrolled in Junior High School 133, which is so brand-new it's not even finished. The teachers unload supplies, check inventories, and I wonder when they'll get around to teaching, but that's okay because it gives me plenty of time to stroll around and hang out with my new friends Lisa, Dolores, and Rita.

Lisa is big and tall with thick, reddish, light-brown hair. She wears tight skirts, sleeveless turtleneck sweaters, trench coats, and carries clutch bags. Her dream is to go to college in Tarrytown, New York, and study to be a detective.

"Where is Tarrytown?" I ask.

"I don't know but you can get there from here," she said.

We hardly ever go to her house because it's full of appliances her brother has stolen from their neighbors. The apartment looks like a warehouse. One time I went to visit, and we took off our coats and threw them onto the plaid sofa. When it was time to leave Lisa shook her coat out and advised me to do the same.

"Why?"

"Roaches."

We always shake out our shoes at my house before putting them on so I knew what she was talking about. We never go to her apartment again.

Dolores is tiny and dark and smart. She found some drug works in her brother's room and told the guidance counselor. I came upon them talking in the hallway between classes.

"Always come to me when there is a problem, Dolores. Always . . ."

Dolores saw me and tried to get away, but the guidance counselor held her tight. Even though she was a little, old, white woman with gray bits of hair, her grip was strong.

"Always," the guidance counselor continued, "always. There is always a solution. I spoke to your parents and it turns out your brother is diabetic. Now isn't that better than what you thought?"

Dolores agreed weakly, pulled away, and ducked into the bathroom, where I found her.

"What's up?" I said.

"Nothing."

We never talk about it and we never go to her apartment, either.

Rita lives on Fox Street around the corner. There is something dark and closed about Fox Street, like it's just a crooked alley off Southern Boulevard and not a street with integrity and a name of its own. Her father hates black people and wears a suit and tie to work every day even though everyone knows he works in a factory. Her mother is a housewife. The one time I visit, Rita's mother has a kerchief tied around her face because the right side of it has collapsed.

"The apartment was really hot," Rita explains. "And when Mami opened the refrigerator the sudden coldness made her face fall."

Since I had been to Rita's house I invite her to mine when Barbra Streisand is going to be on television. I have never seen anyone who looks like Streisand on TV and want Rita to see her, too. But my father comes home dangerous.

"I think I better go," she says.

She never comes back.

Yvonne, I meet in the street. She has quit school and is a little older than me. I go to her house once.

"This is my mother, and Samuel, my stepfather, and these are my two sisters and three brothers."

I wonder where they all sleep because there is only one bedroom.

A young woman comes into the apartment with a little girl.

"Oh, and this is Angela and her little girl, Julie. Mami rents them the bedroom."

So now I know where Yvonne's family sleeps. Wherever they can, all over the living room on cots. There are so many people in that apartment all the time, Yvonne and I hang outside sitting on cars. One day an old man with thin arms and legs and a sharp projectile belly approaches and asks Yvonne where Angela, the woman who rents a room in Yvonne's apartment, is.

"I think she's inside," says Yvonne.

As he turns to go Yvonne whispers, "That's Angela's boyfriend. He pays Mami rent for Angela and Julie to have the bedroom. Angela just has to sleep with him a few times a month for that."

But I stop going there because Angela has the habit of calling her daughter "little whore" and beating her across the legs with a slipper while toilet training her. It's better to socialize in the street or the fire escape.

Ma and I are at the fire escape we share with our Mexican-looking, floor-mopping neighbor. She is not Mexican after all—she is Puerto Rican and her name is Mercedes. She lives with her husband and daughter. They all look alike, squat, long-haired, and like they should live on a farm instead of in the Bronx. Mercedes is sharp but the daughter has a wandering eye and is so lax I often see her tongue resting on the lower lip of her slightly open mouth. I am sitting with my legs dangling through the bars and Ma is sipping coffee and smoking a cigarette when Mercedes joins us at her window.

"How're you doing?" she asks.

"Okay," says Ma self-consciously. Mercedes disapproves of smoking for religious reasons. Her living room is plastered with NO SMOKING signs, making me feel like I've entered a dentist's office whenever I go over there to borrow something. Ma debates in her head whether or not to put out her cigarette when we see a beautiful woman step out of our building and click-clack her way up the street on high heels.

"Look," whispers Mercedes suspiciously. "That's Irena; she lives alone on the other side of the building."

I look down on Irena. She has short, curly hair and is wearing a coral spring coat tied tight to her waist. The hem just hits her big strong calves, which are covered in dark sheer stockings. A boxy handbag dangles from the crook of her elbow and slaps against her hip as she dashes down the street like she has somewhere important to go.

"You know what she does . . ."

But the sight of a small but really handsome man with light, wispy hair coming up the street stops her from finishing her sentence. Mercedes is suddenly confused, disoriented, and I can't decide who I want to know more about, the woman Irena with the coral-color coat and high heels, or the handsome, wispy man! I learn of neither because Mercedes disappears into her apartment and even shuts her window.

"Great, I can smoke," whispers Ma, lighting up.

A few days later Mercedes is in *our* apartment, crying.

"She might be pregnant by now," Mercedes blubbers, one braid coming undone and flapping around. "He always comes back and does . . . this!" She can't go on.

Ma tries to soothe her with coffee.

"And then he leaves her and we don't know what is going on."

"Who is he?" asks Ma.

"Her husband!"

"Her husband?" Ma shoots me a look. "How long has your daughter been married to him?"

I'm surprised to hear that her daughter with the weak eye and lax tongue is married.

"Three years, but he only lived with her one year—and now . . . now . . . he just comes when he has the desire. I'm afraid she'll get pregnant. It's terrible!"

"Why don't they get a divorce?"

Mercedes looks like she has been struck in the face with a dead fish. Then she recoils in horror.

"Because marriage is holy!" she wails.

"Calm down. Calm down," says Ma, thinking, and then adds slowly, "Why do you leave them alone in the apartment?"

"Because married couples need privacy!" says Mercedes, blowing her nose.

Ma suppresses a grin and yearns for but does not reach for a cigarette. I look at Mercedes's flyaway braid and think about her stupid daughter and feel bad that if I had to choose between being like Ma or Mercedes—I'd be like Irena, the pretty woman in the coral coat and high heels, no matter what she does for a living.

CHAPTER 6

Vanessa Delmonte

*H*er hot red panties sizzled like bacon through the bushes . . ." I
am reading *True Confessions* when the prettiest girl I have
ever seen comes knocking at the door.

"*Hola, yo soy Vanessa y vivo en el otro lado.*"

She has two fuzz balls of hair on either side of her head.

"*¿. . . tienen aspirina?*"

She wants aspirin. My mother comes to the door and this girl
explains herself again. Her name is Vanessa Delmonte, she just
moved from Puerto Rico to live with her mother, and she's wondering if we have any aspirin because she has her period and has
cramps.

"Who is your mother?" Ma asks.

"Irena."

My ears perk up. I want to know more about Irena with the high
heels and coral coat. Vanessa smiles; she has a gap between her two
big white teeth, and she makes herself comfortable at the kitchen
table, not minding at all that we stare at her.

"This stone in my navel isn't working to keep the pain away," she
says in Spanish, holding up an orangey-red pebble.

Ma sneaks a look at me. Vanessa's lips are thick but she has the perfect white-person nose. I stare as she begins her story in Spanish after swallowing the pills.

"I used to live with my grandmother in Gurabo, but I got to be too much for her so now she sent me to live with my mother here. I don't know her very well, just met her, really. She sleeps most of the day, anyway . . ."

Ma begins to measure out the rice for dinner. Vanessa jumps up to help.

"I can do that!"

She sorts through the rice, expertly picking out pebbles or tiny rocks. I can tell she knows how to cook.

"I used to cook for my grandmother before she started hiding my clothes."

My father walks in from fixing our car on the people side of the street.

"*Café*," he grunts and goes into the living room.

My mother starts to make coffee. We hear him tuning his guitar and then start to sing. Joe and Petey groan. They had been watching television.

"*Quítame los zapatos.*" My father makes Petey take his shoes off. Petey cries. My mother looks up and spreads her fingers taut to the heavens.

"*Paciencia . . .*" She goes into the living room. "What's going on in here?"

The coffee starts to boil over. Vanessa catches it just in time.

Ma and Petey come back into the kitchen. She sits him down and gives him a cracker, makes the coffee, and puts the water on for the rice. Her mind is elsewhere. But I want to hear more from Vanessa.

"Why did your grandmother hide your clothes?" I ask.

"Who?"

"Your grandmother."

"Because I got too big for her to tie up."

The water for rice starts to boil. Ma lowers the flame, adds some salt and lard. I examine the image of the happy pigs on the green-and-white lard container so I sound casual.

"Why did she tie you up?"

"Why do you think? So I wouldn't go out! But that didn't stop me because there were plenty of sheets."

"Sheets?"

"The sheets she had washed. I always waited for them to dry—then snuck out, grabbed one, and wrapped it around me—like a dress."

Vanessa stays in the kitchen with us until dinner is ready. She's fine just sitting and being quiet and I stare at her perfect nose and her thick two-toned lips and purple gums.

But then—Petey screams; he'd clamped his finger in the electric can opener he'd been playing with and turned on. I pull at his arm weakly. My father races in, screaming, "What the hell is going on?" Ma turns the machine off and releases Petey's finger.

"Come," I say to Vanessa and she follows me into the living room, where Joe has started to wheeze on the sofa.

After bandaging Petey, Ma serves him and my father dinner, and then comes into the living room to ponder Joe. His wheezing is worse. She goes back into the kitchen and serves Vanessa and me. Standing at the stove, she gulps a few mouthfuls of rice and warns my father, *"Ese muchacho ya está sinfónico"* and that if Joe gets any worse they'll have to take him to Lincoln Hospital. Then she blurts out to Vanessa, *"¿Y tu mama? ¿No te está esperando?* You better go home."

"Ma won't be back until tomorrow morning," replies Vanessa in Spanish.

I jump at the chance—"What does your mother do?" I blurt out.

"She works in a bar," says Vanessa and she scurries out as quickly as she scurried in.

The minute she is gone I lock myself in the bathroom and look in the mirror and examine my earlobes, eyes, eyelashes, gums, lips, and teeth. My earlobes are fine, they do not stick out, eyes okay, eyelashes are fine, too, but my gums now seem a little purple. My lips are good, but a little small. I whip my head around suddenly, trying to catch myself unawares, wondering what I would think of my looks if I suddenly came upon myself in the street. There is a knock on the door.

"What?"

"Sonia! *¡Salte del baño! Tenemos que llevar a Joe al hospital.*"

Joe's asthma has gotten worse and he has to be taken to the hospital. I get out of the bathroom.

"*AveMaríaPurísima*, what were you doing in there?" Ma's eyes bug out but I still think about my own face. The minute they are gone I go back to my self-examination. My hair is thick and wavy and considered "good hair," but still I set it on rollers all the time so it will be straighter.

Holding up my hands I quickly flip them—palms, back of hands, palms, back of hands, palms, back of hands, palms, back of hands— looking for a big, shocking difference in color.

A worry I've had since Martin Luther King, Jr., comes up—if I was in the South with light-skinned Little Eddie, would we be separated at a bus stop? Would I have to sit in the back and him in the front? Do strangers think I am a pretty black girl or an ugly white one?

"Go to bed," I yell at Petey, thinking about my purple gums and my fat nose, and I remember a story Ma had heard from her own grandmother about how black people came to be:

In the beginning all people were black because God had made them from the black earth. Then, as a final touch, He made a pool for everyone to dip in and turn white. But there were so many people the water got shallower and shallower, until there were only a few inches of water left. The people at the end of the line had to settle for whitening the soles of their feet, and bending down to place their flat palms in the water, to whiten them, too.

Will I always be at the back of the line?

I fall asleep on the sofa thinking that if Vanessa and I ever blended together we'd make the perfect white girl.

Vanessa is back at our door first thing the next morning.

"Mami is sleeping so we have to be very quiet, but do you want to come over?" she asks. We run over to the other side of the building.

Her mother's apartment is white and gold; white walls and carpeting, white curvy furniture with gold trim—and mirrors everywhere.

"Shhh. Michi . . ." Vanessa shushes a stupid-looking little French poodle named Michelle wearing a diaper.

"Why is she wearing a diaper?"

"Because she has her period."

Does everybody in this house have their period all the time? Vanessa looks like a dark smudge in all that whiteness. We fit better in her room, which is an explosion of color with bright clothes everywhere.

"Do you like this dress?" she says, holding up what looks like a ripped T- shirt. "I made it myself. I can make a lot of clothes. Look."

And we pick through her wardrobe and try on long T-shirts and add bandanas or scarves as belts. Or we take large kerchiefs and twist them around to make halter tops. Sheets make great wraparound skirts, or evening dresses if we pull them up under our armpits.

"When do you clean this room?" I ask her.

She looks at me solemnly and says, "When I can't see the furniture anymore." Then an explosive laugh pops out of her, which makes me laugh, which makes her laugh until we have to throw ourselves on the bed to smother our eruptions and not wake her mother—but it's too late. Irena comes into the room in a white nightgown with feathers around the neck, and on her feet a pair of tight little golden mules.

"*¿Qué está pasando?*" She is immediately bored with us. Vanessa looks around before answering, "Nothing." Vanessa's mom click-clacks into the kitchen to make coffee, her mules slapping her heels warningly. The sound she makes walking makes us want to laugh even harder; when we try to contain ourselves we explode into giggles then choke on them; and that becomes the way we are with each other. Every day we try to make dresses out of kerchiefs and T-shirts.

"Just cut the sleeves off of that T-shirt," she orders.

"Then what?" I ask her.

"Then we wrap it around our heads . . ."

"Like African ladies?"

"Yes, African lady pirates!"

And this makes us fall out laughing and pushing and trying to knock each other over.

When we hang out in the street I see Larry coming and going and avoiding my look. I decide Vanessa and Larry would make a wonderful couple because I want the three of us to be together.

"I think Larry likes you!"

"That *pendejo*?"

"No, really . . ."

When Larry and I are at our windows I twist up.

"I think Vanessa likes you."

He looks surprised, starts to say something, and then stops.

I invite them both to the roof, and then duck out when they get there, or I push her into the hallway when I know he is coming home from school.

No matter what I do, though, Larry always looks bewildered, and Vanessa gets sick of going along with me. And it is all over after I set them up to meet in the courtyard and Larry's father comes upon them, and Larry begins playing handball as if Vanessa isn't there. She is furious and mimics him unable to hit the wall because his knees were quaking: ". . . I tole joo he wuz a fuckin' *pendejo*!"

That summer Larry gets sent away to the Catskills.

It's a long summer with nothing to do so when I don't make clothes with Vanessa, I dig through bins for hot-pink padded bras at discount stores with Yvonne. When the weather finally gets cool, Yvonne and I switch to wearing long pants, and sit on parked cars. Sitting next to her, we look up and down the street looking for something to say.

"There he comes. There he comes!" she says suddenly.

"Who?"

"Mikey . . . it's Mikey . . . we used to date . . . don't look at him."

"Why?"

"I don't want him to think I still like him."

"What?"

"Don't look!"

"Do you?"

"Yes, but his father didn't like me so we had to break up."

"But . . ."

"He loves me but has to make believe he doesn't."

"Why?"

"Shush . . ."

Yvonne never gets Mikey back, and when a young man from Puerto Rico named Luis moves into the neighborhood she starts to go with him.

"Luis is so funny," she says. "The other day we were walking and he took my hand and farted on it."

When I tell Ma about it later I am out on the fire escape and she is at the window having a smoke. "If that's what he does while they are dating, I wonder what he'll do if they get married?" I had not thought of that and it makes me think about the ways of love. Ma's laughing brings Mercedes to her window. Ma rolls her eyes, points to her cigarette, and ducks inside. I sit there awhile, ignoring Mercedes, when the bus pulls up and Larry gets off. He looks stronger, his waist narrow, his legs long, and his shoulders wider. He throws a duffle bag over his shoulder and I get so excited I jump up and down on the fire escape and shake the bars like I am a monkey in a cage.

"Look," I say to Mercedes, "Larry has come back. Larry has come back. Vanessa is going to be so glad to see him!"

"Are you sure *you* are not the one that is so glad to see him?" she says.

Her statement cools me like ice water thrown in my face, and I want to take it all back, but settle for deflating myself and slinking back into the apartment, hoping Larry didn't see.

CHAPTER 7

Back to Square One

'm at the window wondering if Larry will appear, and what do I care anyway?—there was no way we could've been friends—when I hear my sister's voice at the door. Running out to greet her, I see that she and Ma are already gushing all over with talk and I'm still wondering about whether or not I could ever be friends with Larry, so I sneak back to my window to think.

Suddenly I hear my father's strident voice. A flare goes up in my heart and I know to stay frozen right where I am, stuck between the open window with a view of the street and my life. The front door slams and still I wait, immobilized, until out of the corner of my eye I see my sister, shoulders shaking, fleeing down the street and away toward the train. That's my cue to rush toward the kitchen. On my way I spy Petey curling up in the bottom of a closet and Joe rolling under a bed with a baseball bat. In the kitchen Ma is trying to placate my father, and I look to see if she's had time to hide the knives in the oven. She hasn't because this time he has caught her so off guard. Instead, she is heating up a can of peas for dinner like everything is normal. My father is raging, red eyes bugging out, spittle in the corners of his mouth, his anger a notch higher than usual. I block out what he is saying and focus on how the boiling pot of peas could be used as a weapon. Does she know? Would she use it? Would she fling the hot, bubbling peas at him? I telepathically command her to do it while wondering if I could do it myself.

But no matter—my father strikes first by upturning the kitchen table, bending off a leg, and striking her with it. I must have grabbed the black ceramic panther off the television on my way into the fray because it seems to appear in my hand as I bring it up and smash it onto my father's head. It stuns him. Ma takes this second to escape. As she runs past me, my father turns around, graceful as a ballerina, and peers at me and I am sure that he will kill me but he doesn't seem to see me. He looks past me as if I am invisible, then shudders involuntarily like a horse before heading out the door. I lock the door after him but not before seeing our neighbor Mercedes with her mop in hand, peering in. I put up as many pieces of furniture against the door as I can, including the now three-legged kitchen table.

No sooner does he leave than my father starts to try to break back in—smashing his body against the door rhythmically and methodically. I meet Ma in the living room. There is blood running down her face. My brothers have taken up the good hiding places so I put her in the only room with a lock—the bathroom. Once she is so obviously hidden, I pick up the very weapon he had hit her with, the table leg, and stand in the hallway, waiting for him to come crashing through.

Focusing on the rose pattern printed on the linoleum floor I notice how a big, lush, red flower opens up to a stem, which leads to another flower. In my head, I follow a pattern of sight and sound: the roses and the thuds my father makes against the door. Hear a thud, see a rose, hear a thud, and see a rose, until the rose pattern crashes against the wall as my father comes bursting through the door. But two big Irish cops come rushing in right after him. Mercedes is in the hallway peering in, and I don't mind because I figure it was she who called the cops.

"Okay, calm down . . . that's it . . ." says one cop, looking at my father but really looking at his partner.

"She no suppose to do what she want," my father says, stumbling around, shaking like a horse trying to clear its head.

"That's all right now," answers the other cop.

I get my mother out of the bathroom.

"Arrest him," she says. "Look what that *abusador* did!" She points to her head and the broken furniture.

"Lady, we can't arrest him. We didn't see him commit any acts of violence. Now look, why don't you get a restraining order . . . ?"

What? I can't believe it. They go back and forth about a restraining order, and how they can't arrest him because they didn't see him committing any acts of violence, and how much trouble it would be to press charges, and why doesn't everybody just calm down, and I start to shake, and continue to shake and begin to cry, but no sound comes out so nobody notices. The cops take him out, insisting he clear his head, and I must've attended to Ma's wound but I can't be sure. I only know that time passed.

Over the next few days the family settles down around me. My father fixes the leg back onto the table. Joe wheezes asthma and Petey weeps, and Ma yells at us to come to dinner—everyone gets back to normal, except for me. I cannot stop crying and even sit at the dinner table, tears streaming down my face, with Ma looking away and Pops looking at my forehead until they both get sick of me.

"*¿Qué diablo te pasa?*" they finally ask.

"I can't!" I sob. "I can't take this anymore!"

My parents look at each other like I've lost my mind.

"Can't take what?" my mother asks, rolling her eyes.

Did I hear right? Does she not know what I'm talking about? Is she joking? Has she forgotten what had happened? The cops! The broken kitchen table! The bump on the head! Christ. My mouth moves as I try to talk but I am so flabbergasted nothing comes out. Besides, I would explode with words if I could figure out what to say to her.

She looks to Pops, who seems like he just got amnesia, too. Then she turns back to me. "Oh, that—that had nothing to do with you," she says with great exasperation. My father scratches his head like he has no idea what either one of us is talking about.

They are in cahoots and leave the room, taking the air with them. I deflate but then inflate, thinking, *Screw them. I'm going to run away like kids do on television. That'll show 'em.* But where to? I know—I'll go to my sister's. I can be safe there. No, not my sister's. I don't know this but I feel it as sure as I can feel an undertow in the ocean—her relationship with my father does not make her place neutral territory. I hide the fact that I'm too much of a coward to put her between my parents and me, and decide to run away to my grandmother's house in El Barrio.

"*Perate, perate, perate,*" says my grandmother, motoring around the apartment. I follow her into the kitchen. Using her calloused fingers as pot holders she shoves the lid off a pot of rice. It falls to the side with a clatter. I expect her to ask me what I am doing there but she doesn't; instead she stirs the rice, flips the lid up in the air with her knuckles, and coaxes it back onto the pot.

We sit in the dining room. Me with a tragic look on my face and hoping she asks me for details as to why I've shown up, but she doesn't. After her smoke she decides to check if the beans are hot.

"Ahhhhhgggggg!"

They're hot. I run in as she soaks her burned hand in cool water. When she pulls her hand out, I impulsively kiss the burned part. This surprises her almost as much as my action surprises me. She pulls her hand away in shock and looks at me suspiciously. That night I bed down with La Boba, whose serene smile helps me sleep.

When I get back to the block days later I know Vanessa knows everything without me even telling her. Not only that, she's come up with a plan.

"Don't worry, I can make him stop drinking!" She grins.

"How?" I ask.

"Santería..."

I know of this spiritual practice of putting spells on people and other voodoo stuff. Bon Bon always leaves food or shots of whiskey out for her spirits and slaps babies to ward off the evil eye, so we go to a *botánica,* half seriously and half not, and look over the prayers that are set up on a rack like greeting cards.

"Here, this one will make someone fall in love with you," she says in a deadpan voice, shoving me. "Here is one that will make you rich, and this one will make you famous." The silliness of buying something to make me rich and famous makes me laugh so hard the owner, who is all dressed in white, comes out from the back.

"What's so funny?" she says.

Vanessa seriously explains that we want a prayer to make my father stop drinking. The owner pulls a box out from behind the counter, leafs through it, and pulls out a flyer and a candle. "You have to buy this candle, too," she says sternly. We buy what we need and wait until we get outside to laugh.

The prayers and candle don't work.

But our attempt gives me an idea. The back pages of *True Confessions* feature lots of advertisements. You could send away for "Frownies" to take away wrinkles just like movie stars do, or you can send away for vitamins to make you stop being a ninety-five-pound weakling, or, what really catches my eye, pills you can secretly put in your husband's drink to make him stop drinking. I show Vanessa.

"Let's send for everything," she says. "We can take away his wrinkles, make him get fat and stop drinking, too!"

"No, just the anti-drinking stuff," I say. And laughing and knocking each other over we send away for it. When it arrives we show Ma in the kitchen.

"What do you think, Ma? Let's try it in coffee; he always drinks coffee."

We make coffee with sugar and milk just the way he likes it, and put the pills in and wait. Though doubtful, even Ma looks over. Everything looks okay until the cup starts to bubble over like an Alka-Seltzer. Ma sniffs and goes back to what she was doing, and Vanessa and I laugh until our eyes tear.

"We can go back to the *botánica* and ask about sacrificing a chicken," Vanessa suggests.

"*AveMaríaPurísima*," says Ma.

We look to each other for what to do next and go to a running joke between us—which one of us might have more African ancestors. A sure sign is having purplish gums. We examine hers first.

"Now yours," she says, giggling.

We do. Then we examine our hair, our skin, our features, and laughing so hard about a forbidden topic makes everything bad go away for a while.

———

The trip to the Catskills has made Larry bolder. Not even afraid to talk to Puerto Ricans in public, so I am not so shocked to see him at a party on Fox Street with Vanessa. There's lots of couples dancing and drinking beer and I am dancing with a boy named Johnny who is Spanish and tall and Indian-looking with long, thin hair.

Suddenly a guy throws up near us. Everybody screams in disgust, but the guy's girlfriend rushes to clean up the vomit, proving to everyone that she is his woman and he is her man. When she is done cleaning and helping her man out the door, Johnny pulls me back into his arms and we dance and out of the corner of my eye I see Vanessa and Larry dancing, too. Larry has one hand on the small of her back, and the other hand squeezes her breast as she yawns in his face. They are excluding Johnny and me even though they are not really with each other. Suddenly I want to leave the party.

"Hey, wait, don't go," says Johnny.

But I want to go.

"I'll walk you home then."

Johnny walks me home more and more often, and he becomes my boyfriend because he is just tall enough to make me feel cute. He comes to visit me when I am alone in the apartment, but I am afraid. Not because he will kiss me or touch me or want me to touch him, but because of who I turn into whenever he comes over.

I put on a housedress like my mother and do the laundry! Then I want to serve him rice and beans and kiss his hands. Where on earth did I get that idea that it was sexy to do that with a boy? I hope it was from a Sophia Loren movie and not from my mother! Wherever I got it, I don't like it.

And it gets worse. I start going to church with him because that's the place all young ladies in love go to be with their boyfriends so we can bump our breasts against their arms accidentally-on-purpose on the way there.

"It's quits!" I tell him one day when I've had enough.

"Why?" He is astounded.

"Don't think I am ever going to clean up your vomit," I tell him.

"What?"

"Your vomit! I don't play that . . ."

"But I don't even feel sick . . . ?"

"It's quits anyway."

"What?"

"You heard me, it's over!"

"But what's the matter?"

"Never mind, it's just quits," I answer.

And I run like the wind.

CHAPTER 8

Worlds Collide

A y, *Dios mío . . . !*" My mother comes home crying, distraught.

My heart jumps and I look for my father behind her. But he isn't there; it's something else.

"What happened?"

"Your sister is living with a man!"

I am relieved now.

"You *idiota*, she'll get pregnant and he'll leave her!"

I think it's romantic. My sister *has* changed; she's grown her hair long, wears casual clothes, everything is looser about her, somehow. She's even quit her job and her neat-looking roommate and blond furniture to live on the Lower East Side like a poor person again. I decide to visit her and her boyfriend. The streets I walk along on the way over from the train are filthy, garbage everywhere, bodegas galore. It reminds me of my old neighborhood on Third Avenue. *Why live here?* I wonder. She graduated high school and has a good job as a keypunch operator for Eastern Airlines. I enter the building and there's a girl trying to get up the stairs ahead of me. She has a baby in one arm and is dragging a four-year-old up the stairs with the other hand.

"*¡Avanza, zángano!*" She screams at a little boy to hurry up. He tries to, but falls, so she smacks him on the head. He howls, the girl's mother comes out of an apartment in a housedress and rollers, and I can see through the door even more kids crying on saggy sofas decorated with dirty lace.

"*¿Qué pasa?*" yells the mother.

"Here." The girl tosses the baby to her and then threatens the little boy, smacking him on his butt. "I'll give you a reason to cry!" Finally they all tumble into their apartment, where I hear their muffled troubles go on. I wonder again, why live here?

Entering my sister's apartment I'm still surprised at how long she has let her hair grow. A man is at the door. "Come on in . . ." It's her tall white boyfriend from Mississippi, Bill. "Have a seat."

I like him right away because he has an easy, drawly way of talking.

"How's Ma?" asks my sister.

"She's worried . . . I guess."

"She should worry about herself . . ."

"Yeah . . . I guess."

There are books on cinder-block bookcases, and lots of plants, and posters, records, and colorful candles that drip wax onto Chianti wine bottles, nothing at all like the apartment I had just peeked into next door. Classical music is drifting all around me as she settles down and continues to work on a mobile of tiny plastic airplanes. Bill looks around uncertainly. "I'm heading out for beer," he announces and leaves. There is a big cat lounging on the metal panel covering the tub in the kitchen and I remember my mother cooking my father in a similar one, so long ago.

I am left with this new sister who asks me carefully, "How are things?"

"Fine."

"Are you sure?"

"Yeah, I'm sure . . ."

"Good, because I was afraid you were losing your spirit."

"My spirit?"

"Yes, and Joe and Petey, too."

"They are losing their spirit?"

"Yeah . . ."

I wonder if I should change my shoelaces.

"You guys should look out for each other," she adds.

I can't stand my brothers, but I am afraid to say so.

"Especially Joe. Because he is in the middle of you three."

I hear the children cry next door.

She pauses, then adds, "Ma's not a saint, you know. She has problems . . ."

I look at the mobile Aurea's building and how carefully balanced it all is.

"She lives that way because she wants to, you know . . ."

The little plastic planes are all the same but they are different colors, and she's managing to make them go in all different directions.

"Ma made her bed, and now she has to sleep in it."

One misplaced plane could send it all to hell.

"You can't help her, you know . . ."

I hand her the next plane and wonder how she'll hang it without them all crashing into each other.

"Here's five bucks. Go find a dance class somewhere."

I take the five dollars and feel guilty I am jealous that she cares about Joe and Petey, too.

———

White neighbors who have small children named Dylan and Donovan come over. Later, more friends stop by. They are all *Americanos*. Are they hippies or beatniks? They smoke and drink a lot of beer while they play guitar and sing songs around the kitchen table.

It's dark as a dungeon way down in the mine.

What mines? What people dying in Appalachia of black lung disease? They drink more beer.

Tura lura lura
Tura lura lye
Tura lura lura
That's an Irish lullaby.

What sad songs they sing. But the sadder the songs the happier the beer makes them. Dinner is spiced ham-and-cheese sandwiches, which I eat in the jungle of plants hanging in the living room, sitting on the mattress on the floor, careful not to get mayonnaise on the Indian bedspread, and listening.

"Women around here have babies to prove their femininity, not 'cause they want them . . ."

"Black people and white people are much closer in the South. I mean, they are actually in each other's lives. Here in the north the black man might be free but totally isolated . . . !"

"You can't compare Faulkner to Hemingway . . ."

"Why is Baldwin always left out of the equation . . . ?"

"At least the English introduced the concept of legal systems to the New World. In South America the Spanish introduced machismo, belligerence, and an idiotic religion."

"Play some Miles, will you . . . ?"

I wonder what all they are talking about. Who is Faulkner . . . and Baldwin, and all the others? What kind of talking is this that is not really an argument? This talk has no winners or losers, only exchanges. I want to know what Vanessa would make of all this and can't wait to bring her around.

"Wait'll you see, Vanessa. It's a cheap apartment. I'm sure we can get one when we graduate high school. I'm going to be a secretary and you'll be something, too," I tell her on the train over. "Wait until you see. We can decorate it with books and plants . . ."

We get out of the train station and head east. Vanessa picks up a cigarette butt from the street and smokes it. At my sister's she stands around blankly.

"Look at this book! Look at this macramé! Look at this . . ."

"Can we go soon?" she asks.

"But listen to this African woman who sings by clicking her tongue . . . !"

But Vanessa is bored and her silence urges us to go. On the train I feel stuck and frozen between two places, two worlds, two ways of seeing things.

"Come over, we'll make a dress for tomorrow," she says when we get to our building.

"Later," I say, deciding on going my own way, to my side of the building. In the apartment Joe is wheezing on the bed and Ma tells me to sit with him at the window. My father comes home, sees what's going on, and tries to help the situation.

"*¡Mal rayo te parta!*" he screams up to God, shaking his fist.

Joe hunches over more and adds a moan to his rattling.

"*Cálmate,*" warns Ma excitedly.

"Calm down," she says. But I can't tell if she is trying to calm Joe or my father.

Joe's chest heaves up as his stomach deflates to almost touch his spine. I count his ribs. My parents argue in the living room. I close the door to the room so my brother can rattle in peace. Finally my raging father and my supplicating mother take Joe to Lincoln Hospital. When they return it's my mother who is raging, exasperated with the list of foods Joe should avoid.

"Peanut butter," my mother shrieks. "What Puerto Ricans eat peanut butter?"

I hear them talking into the night, and the next day, and the next. I gather through innuendo and some eavesdropping that someone is going on a trip. Who? It's Joe. He's going to be sent to Puerto Rico.

"For how long?" I ask.

"Till he gets better," my mother emphatically states. "If he stays here he'll die for sure."

So far the existence of Puerto Rico has been like background noise, a mostly bad place of a hunger and sadness that inspires beautiful songs. But all of a sudden Puerto Rico is front and center and is going to save Joe's life.

"Who is he going to live with?" I want to know.

"With my father . . ."

I can't believe it. "You are sending Joe to be with your father? I thought your father was a mean *sinvergüenza*."

"Not just my father, my father and his wife, who is nice. You know, when I was your age I went to see them and I wanted to look good so I made a skirt with a kick pleat in the back. Before I could even say '*Hola*,' he slapped me so hard for wearing that skirt I fell off the porch."

"And that was *nice*?"

"Let me finish. His wife was there and she said, 'Dionisio, you should not have done that.'"

"That makes it okay?"

"Never mind," she snaps.

And so she dresses Joe in a little suit and sends him to that other world I have always heard so much about, Puerto Rico.

CHAPTER 9

Agitation

Get out of the bathroom!" screams Ma.

But I can't. I am so beautiful and sexy I can't tear myself away from the mirror. I have even grown to love my breasts because they are soft and curvy and their size makes my waist look tiny. "Wait a second," I yell back. "Almost done," I say before taking a deep breath, closing my mouth, and applying enough hair spray to choke a goat.

"Come on . . . !"

I give myself one last spritz and open the door. Ma rushes in.

"What the hell . . ." she says, waving her arms around in the fog of hair spray. "*AveMaríaPurísima*, you're going to go blind!"

"Ma, should I cut my hair?"

"What?"

"My hair . . ."

"Your hair? Were you looking at your hair all this time? We've got to go! Are you crazy? I can't believe you've been combing your hair all this time! Your father can't start the car, you know!"

"What do I care?" I mutter under my breath.

"*Mira . . .*" she warns me, but before she can go on my father comes in the door wearing three sweatshirts. He looks through me and I wonder why he doesn't have a coat. The sweatshirts are short in the sleeves, and ride up and stretch across his belly.

"We got a dead battery . . . I gotta get a boost . . ."

They start to argue and I look into the mirror to make sure of my existence then follow them, tumbling out the door and into the car, as my father fumbles around under the hood of our clunker and the jalopy helping us. Sitting in the rear I stare at the back of my father's head, his ears sticking out, and I remember how he used to wiggle them to make me laugh when I was little and I scratched his back, acres wide. Now the lines in his neck are deep and undulate between his outbursts of rage and bewilderment at his faulty car. His sweatshirts are ripped and frayed at the neck. He does not wear gloves though it's cold out, and his bare hands seem too thick to curl around the steering wheel. I wonder how he manages to play guitar. These thoughts linger all day at school and that night, desperate to relieve myself of a gnawing desire to understand my father, I ask him to teach me to play guitar.

"What?" he says, surprised.

"I want to play."

He looks at me like I'm speaking a foreign language. Then his eyes focus.

"You?"

"Yes, me. I want to play."

Awkwardly he teaches me three chords. So I begin practicing and even buy the Joan Baez songbook, but I don't really want to play her songs, the songs my sister and her friends sing about people working in mines and dying of black lung disease, or lovers named Mattie Grove beheaded by Scottish kings for sleeping with Scottish queens. I want to play Puerto Rican *aguinaldos*. We've got songs about starving workers and murderous lovers, too. I practice playing and singing four lines of an *aguinaldo* about people crashing each other's Christmas parties, until the tips of my fingers form calluses a bit like my father's. When I think I'm good enough to have somebody listen I wait for Pops to come home in an okay mood and I sit in the living room and play and sing.

En esta parranda
Venimos cantando . . .

"Let me have that guitar," he says, taking it out of my hands. "It's not even tuned." He tunes it and begins to play and sing himself. I wait, but by the time he gets to the second verse of his song, he has forgotten me, and I wander over to the window wanting to jump out of my skin, bothered with hopes and wants that I would go after in a minute because I am not afraid—but I can't go after something I can't even define, now, can I? I look out and up, hoping that Larry is there, but he hardly comes to the window now.

"Come and eat!" Ma yells.

"I don't want to. I'm not hungry," I yell back.

She comes into the room. "Growing pains," she says smugly, *"AveMaríaPurísima,"* and leaves.

And that sends me over the top. Who is *she* to use psychological babble when *she's* the one who hides knives in the oven when it gets dark on Friday nights and my father isn't home yet?

The months drag by and one day at school I am so annoyed by a tune I can't get out of my head, I do my nails.

"How many of you are going to the World's Fair?" the teacher asks us while I furtively apply the first coat. "It's not far, just Queens, you should all get your parents to take you."

Lisa and I look at each other.

"What a great idea. Why don't we ask them to take us to the moon while we're at it?" I whisper.

We snicker as I put on the final coat of polish and walk around the classroom to dry them. The tune from *Swan Lake* I heard the weekend before at my sister's house is still driving me crazy and before I know it I blurt out, "Hey, Teach, who wrote *Swan Lake*? Tchaikovsky or Toscanini?"

"Who?"

"Tchaikovsky or Toscanini?"

"How do you know about those people?"

"I don't. That's why I'm asking you."

"It was Tchaikovsky. Toscanini is still alive and he is a conductor and a composer."

"Oh . . ."

"So tell me, how do you know about them?"

"My sister told me."

Teach is astounded. "Come help me unpack paper supplies."

I begin to help him every day, and I don't mind because it gives me something to do and he's trapped enough to answer all my questions. I want to know something about *Hamlet*. Aurea played a record of it for me the weekend before and all I can remember is how emotional I thought it was, though the actor had the most nasally voice I had ever heard.

"That's Richard Burton you were listening to."

"Yeah, I know, but I'm not sure I get his problem."

Teach tells me how Hamlet doesn't know what to do about suspecting that his uncle killed his father in order to marry his mother.

"Shakespeare must've been part Puerto Rican to come up with that one."

The next day I help him some more.

"You want to know something?" he says out of nowhere.

"What?"

"Of all the kids here, you will be one of the few who won't get pregnant or end up on drugs."

Suddenly I am angry. Why is he telling me something about myself? How does he know what I am going to do? Let him unpack his own damn stuff. And I go to the back of the class with Lisa and Dolores to put on eyeliner and talk about how much we hate the Beatles.

"What a stupid song that is . . . 'I Want to Hold Your Hand,'" says Dolores.

"Yeah, the guys I know want to hold something else," cracks Lisa. We laugh.

"They're going to be on television Sunday . . ."

"Who?"

"The Beatles!"

"Forget about them," I say. I'm itching for something but I don't know what, and I add, "Let's figure out a way to go to the World's Fair," but my friends ignore me.

I'm setting my hair in rollers while I watch *The Ed Sullivan Show*, figuring I can sit through the Beatles until the acrobats come on. But the Beatles don't come on—they explode on the screen with a shimmering freshness and promise of possibilities and new things to come. I almost poke myself in the eye with a hairpin. The phone rings right after the Beatles sing "I Want to Hold Your Hand." It's Lisa.

"Oh my God, Sonia!"

"I know . . . !"

"They were . . ."

"I know—I can't believe it." My hand shakes, I am so excited. Suddenly it's absolutely necessary we go to the World's Fair.

"Lisa, let's go to the World's Fair."

I hear her pause on the other end of the line. "When?"

"Tomorrow! We've got to go tomorrow." I try to steady my voice but unexplainable tears threaten to betray me.

She says it slowly but it's what I want to hear. "Okay . . ."

"We'll play hooky. They won't even notice."

"Okay, meet at the subway . . ."

Twelve hours later we're on the train. Now if we can only find Queens. We go uptown, downtown to Forty-Second Street, but get confused that there are two Forty-Second Streets, east and west. Hours later we finally get to the World's Fair and are starving so we share a pretzel because it's all we can afford.

"Look, here is a list of all the free exhibits," I say.

Unfortunately all the free exhibits are the crappy ones. Still—we don't care. We wander around and before we know it it's one forty-five and we have to be back by three.

"Oh no! We've got to go!" I say.

Running into the train station we begin our journey, jerking forward and backward to the Bronx because we've retained no information about how we got to the Fair in the first place and get just as lost heading back. Finally, after hours and hours, we stumble upon a familiar train station.

"This is it!" cries Lisa.

Standing on the station we look at each other triumphantly. We don't have the words but we feel great because we did it!

"Oh my God, Sonia!"

"I know . . . !"

"We did it . . ."

"I know—I can't believe it."

Suddenly we sing, "*. . . summer's here and the time is right for dancin' in the street . . .*" And it's so funny that we started warbling at the same exact moment we press cheeks together, slap each other five, and run out of the station, thrilled that we went somewhere.

CHAPTER 10

Down with Puerto Rico

Judging by the way Joe looks when he comes back from Puerto Rico months later, I think my parents did the right thing in sending him there.

"Hey, Joe!" I say.

He smiles.

"*Ay, gracias a Dios . . .*" says my mother. She helps him out of his little suit.

"I'll make coffee," she says, flitting into the kitchen.

Pops says nothing but I think he is happy, because he follows her.

Joe takes a deep breath, and then another. I smile at him but he doesn't smile back. His next breath comes on a little quicker.

"Let's go into the room," I say.

We do and by the time we get there his breath starts coming on super fast.

"Joe?"

He says nothing but starts gasping. I can't believe he's having an asthma attack! He's filled out. He looks so good. But why is he sick? I look at the corner of the bed, the wall, pick up a magazine, then put it down. I try not to hear. I wonder what Larry is doing upstairs, but before I know it, I find myself sitting with Joe at the window just like in the old days. He tries to suck up the air, and it's as if he never left town. Ma hears and comes in wild-eyed. "This is my cross to bear," she wails.

"*¡Mal rayo te parta!*" screams my father.

But they leave us alone for a moment.

"Joe," I ask carefully, "do you want to go back to Puerto Rico? Did you like it better there? You didn't get sick there. Maybe you should go back. They'll send you back . . . if you want to go . . . You looked great in the pictures they sent . . . always in a suit . . . always slightly smiling . . ." And then my spiel is cut short when in the exact same theatrical way a blind person who finally accepts God flings off his black glasses and screams, "I can see! I can see!" or the way a cripple crawls up to an altar then flings his crutches away in a moment of epiphany and screams, "I can walk! I can walk!" my brother's attack ends in midgasp.

But we are not done with Puerto Rico. I find myself roiled in foul imaginings of the island when Ma announces that she and I will visit. "Down with Puerto Rico! Revenge on the island! Screw those people!" becomes my internal battle cry as I vow to shun and reject the place I've never been to, where kids drown in sewage, the place of dead mothers, of negligent fathers, of starvation and poverty, of macho men throwing coconuts at their wives' heads for fun! I know of all the horrors even beautiful songs written about the island can't cover up and will not be fooled by it.

I'll even expose my grandfather for the rat he is. One look from me and he'll know that I don't play that way, and that I *know* how he kicked Ma down the stairs for wearing a nice skirt and that he cheated on my grandmother Encarnación Falcon, the saintly angel, and then abandoned his kids as soon as she died.

Who did they think they were, making Ma work like a slave just so she could eat? I know all about those mongooses she had to navigate through and her terror of being spackled into a wall and about the urine she had to drink.

Of course my mother had to pick Manhattan over this dumb island, and I am going to get a high school diploma to prove she did the right thing. Maybe they could beat down an orphan girl like her but not me, because I was born in the USA. I'll show those hicks up.

Vanessa arms me with a white sheath dress and I wear my hair in a French twist to meet the enemy. We land in San Juan and I get ready to fight—but the Puerto Rican air ambushes me. It stops me in my tracks as it sweeps through me disguised as "breeze." How was I to know it was going to be balmy, sweet, perfumed, delightful, erotic, warm, and make me happy to perspire just so? Still, I am determined to remain sullen. A half brother of Ma's, Rafa, picks us up at the airport and asks, "How are things?"

"*¿Y qué, Isa? ¿Como están las cosas?*"

Ma answers, "In the struggle."

"*Ya vez, todavía luchando.*"

He asks after my father.

"*¿Y Manzano?*"

"*Como siempre.*"

"Like always"? I listen—what did that mean, my father was "like always"? Did they know about my father? Was the way my father acted part of being Puerto Rican?

Hibiscus flowers growing over, around, even through chain-link fences bordering the roadway undermine my determination to "show them up" even more. I'm rendered even more useless by the *flamboyan* trees with perky pink flowers standing at attention that remind me of my fifteen-year-old nipples, and then by the mangos and other fruit I can't identify that resemble private parts, and then by giant philodendrons waving to me as we drive by. Christ, I can't even think! I'm dizzy, drunk on extreme sensory overload, and I try sobering up by listening to Ma and Rafa's conversation, but the next question is directed toward me.

"*¿Y qué, Sonia?*"

Once again I am surprised at how much Spanish I know. I answer in Spanish.

"I'm fine. *Bien.*"

"It's great to finally meet you."

"Does Puerto Rico have any great places like Coney Island?" I ask bitterly.

"I don't think so."

"Did you know that millions of people go to Coney Island on Fourth of July weekend?"

"I didn't know that." He grins.

"Not only that, you can buy a Sabrett hot dog almost anywhere."

"You don't say . . ."

"And chocolate egg creams. Can you get a chocolate egg cream in Puerto Rico?"

But then I forget what I'm showing off about because we turn onto a road along a beach, and the turquoise and blues of the Caribbean Sea make me dumb. On the rest of the ride I wonder how

I could have been told that Adam and Eve were thrown out of paradise, which was no more. Well, paradise is right here.

Finally Rafa points out my grandfather's house on a wide, shady street as we park a ways from it. The hot sunlight creates lacy patterns on the sandy ground as it shoots through the plants, reminding me of the patterns created by the sun through the Third Avenue El. As we walk toward the house, neighbors come out to meet and greet us, and I am struck that their skin tones really are *canela, trigueña, negrita,* just like the songs say. The people are caramel color with light eyes and wavy, long, black hair, chocolate color with kinky blond hair and olive-black eyes. Is it the sun? Do we not look like this in New York because our skins turn generic gray with cold?

I finally come face-to-face with Ma's first tormentor.

My grandfather could play an elder Picasso in a movie. Short, bald, barrel-chested, and wearing Bermuda shorts, a white athletic undershirt, and brown rubber sandals. He looks like he has been bleached and tanned by the sun so many times his original color is gone. He has some spots but I can't tell if he is a dark man with light spots or vice versa. I try looking into his face as Ma coaxes me into giving him a hug. I don't notice him giving *her* a hug. He gave her an impersonal jostle. Our hug is like accidentally bumping into someone.

He seems totally self-contained, solitary, and like a rock in the middle of a river—things seem to float around him.

"*Hola, Sonia.*"

"*Hola.*"

"*¿Qué tal?*"

"*Bien, bien.*"

Then to Ma.

"Hola, Isa."

"Hola."

"¿Qué tal?"

"Bien, bien."

After a few days I become aware that he never gives way or extends himself. You could be there or not; he never takes notice. He speaks when spoken to but never offers any information or asks any questions. You are free to stay or go as you please. He sleeps in his own room on a full-size bed that is pushed against the wall under a window.

"Mira como hace su cama," Ma whispers to me.

Ma is fascinated by how he makes his bed, so I watch him do it as well. Every morning he adjusts the sheets and light blanket with the tip of his cane, before arranging the mosquito net out of the way for the day.

Ma and Dionisio don't talk much—not even about Joe's rehabilitative visit. My grandfather's wife and daughters quickly fill in the empty spaces his attitude leaves with listless chatter, and soon his stepson, Rafa, steps in by coming around two or three days later and insisting we stay with him and his wife in Bayamón. We say goodbye to Dionisio.

"Adiós, Sonia."

"Adiós."

"Hasta luego."

"Sí."

Then to my mother.

"Adiós, Isa."

"Adiós."

"Hasta luego."

"*Sí.*"

Rafa's wife runs a dress factory that makes beautiful, sexy clothes "suited to the Latin woman," she says. She has green eyes and caramel skin and sometimes her hair is curly and sometimes it is straight.

"How do you make it straight?" I ask.

She gestures toward the ironing board in her sewing room. "Come and kneel down in front of the board." I do and she loosens my hair and grabs a strand of it.

"What are you doing?"

"Be still . . ."

Laying my hair on the board she irons it! And after twenty minutes of contorting my body around I have a head of stick-straight hair. Then we talk about favorite television shows, even particular episodes we have both seen, and I begin to feel Puerto Rico is not very backward at all.

But when we go to the countryside to visit Ma's older sister, Cristina, Puerto Rico flips back in time and I see a glimpse of what Ma always talks about. Cristina is cooking at a charcoal stove in a shed at the back of her house, soot covering her hands and face.

"Don't hug me." She smiles up at Ma. "You'll get like me!"

Ma doesn't care and I can see the blend of sorrow and pleasure on her face as she hugs her anyway. They squeeze, then step away long enough to examine each other before crushing together again.

"*¡Tanto tiempo . . . !*"

I look at Cristina and place her in the stories my mother has told me. My aunt is plump and wears a loose housedress and rubber sandals just like the ones my grandfather wears. Her hair is slightly gray and pulled in a tight, substantial bun. Her hands are thick, her nails grimy. My mother introduces me.

"Mi hija, Sonia . . ."

My aunt hugs me and I look into her face, so similar to my mother's—except where my mother's eyes are impatient, my aunt's are calm and serene with a sweetness in her gaze that overwhelms me as it covers my mother with joy, as if she had last seen her a hundred years ago or yesterday. We walk inside and see the main room is festooned with her grandchildren. Babies and toddlers in dripping diapers ramble around a floor with huge holes in it. Later, in the quiet of the mountains, my mother pulls Cristina's husband of more than thirty years aside and counsels him. "You must cover the holes in the floor of your house. There is no reason to live this way anymore. Think of the children."

"But the children know where the holes are by now," he answers seriously.

But it is in this interior of the mountains that Puerto Rico grabs my heart. A magic mist floats around the greenery of it all, making the plantain leaves and red, red earth mysterious, and the sound of all the roosters crowing in the mornings is comically droll and arresting. My mother looks different to me.

"When I stayed with Mama Santa, a grandmother, we used to get up in the morning and gather herbs for her *remedios,*" Ma tells me. "And then we used to grind coffee together. She always had her head wrapped up in a scarf and wore necklaces, and bracelets that jangled on her arms, making sounds I used to love . . ." In my imagination my mother looks sweet as a barefoot little girl with red dirt coming up between her toes and a raggedy dress on.

I take inventory of all my mother's siblings: Uncle Eddie, who had suffered so much on the island he vowed never to return; Uncle Frank, who followed Ma to New York; Cristina, who stayed on the island. There is one more to meet, Félix, the one whose urine my mother was forced to drink. I am shocked by his handsomeness. Very tall, with chiseled features. He has been with the same woman, his wife, Minerva, since they were both fourteen-year-old children and sold fried foods from a pushcart to make ends meet.

He hugs Ma and looks over her shoulder at me and we giggle. His wife is very black and they have three children, and he will do anything to make them laugh. He loves to tease her.

"These plantains you cooked look like they were run over by a truck!"

But he and I don't need a gag or a joke to laugh over—we laugh for no reason at all, communicating in broken English and Spanish.

When it is finally time to return to New York, we stop on the way to the airport when Uncle Félix spots a roadside vendor selling coconuts. My mouth waters as the vendor picks a coconut, slices off the top with a dangerous-looking machete, sticks a straw in it, and hands it to me. I am disappointed that it tastes weak and watery, not like the canned Coco López coconut milk I had imagined.

I leave the island longing for Puerto Rico with the phantom ache of an amputee who still feels his missing arm.

CHAPTER 11

My Dramatic Life

The new drama teacher wants to put up a board illustrating all the wonderful theater he is going to introduce us to.

"The title of our board will be, 'Drama Is Everyday Living.'"

"How about, 'Drama Is Life'?" I suggest.

"Yes," he agrees. "That is better. I sound like a teacher, don't I?"

"Yes."

I am surprised that he speaks to me without the tone of correction in his voice, and the next morning I decide to dress more grown-up. I wear my hair in a French twist, and iron a white blouse to wear with a black jumper.

"Who would like to help with the board?" he asks.

I raise my hand immediately.

"Okay, cut out these letters to say, 'Drama Is Everyday Living.'"

I thought he had liked my idea of saying "Drama Is Life" and wonder what changed his mind. Maybe my idea wasn't *that* good after all. But he *did* notice me for a second. Maybe I can make him notice me again. How to do that? I decide to wear tight sweaters. He plays a recording of the Broadway show *Oliver!* and asks us to listen to the lyrics of a song.

I'm surprised that it's a love song about a woman who is beaten by her lover, who is a cruel thief. (At least my father isn't a thief.)

The teacher loves this song. It's weird. What's going on with this? What's so great about clinging on to a man who beats you? Why do people find it entertaining? He announces we're going to do a production of a few of the songs.

"Will you write a couple of scenes to get into the songs?" he asks me. Me? Why me? Was it the tight sweater? I write a scene where Oliver Twist talks about his mother dying:

Oliver: She went . . . (Oliver looks up to the sky) . . . you know.

"Hmmm . . ." says the drama teacher. Then he reads it out loud, ridiculing it with mimicry in his voice, then adds, "A little corny, don't you think?" *Screw you,* I think. I've never done this before! But I stick with it.

Months later the drama teacher tells me he thinks I should audition for the High School of Performing Arts.

"What's that?" I ask.

"A special school in Manhattan, part of the New York City school system. It's for artists like musicians, and dancers, and actors. You would audition for acting."

"What's 'audition'?"

"A tryout, and if they like you, you go there."

"I don't know if my parents would let me."

"I'll go ask them myself."

"What?"

"What time are you done with dinner?"

"Seven thirty."

"I'll be there at eight."

And he is. Right on time. He comes over and tells my parents about Performing Arts. My father looks on stonily. Ma listens unsurely and quickly agrees that I can attend Performing Arts if I get in. I can tell they are uncomfortable with having a white teacher in their living room and want to get rid of him as soon as possible, but I feel uncomfortable that they agree with him so quickly. They don't know him that well.

To prepare for my audition we practice a monologue about a woman whose husband got shot by Nazis.

"Now, when you say, 'and they shot him,' I want you to really feel it."

"Like how?"

"Like this." He demonstrates by squishing up his face and curling his upper lip into a snarl.

I squish up my face and curl my upper lip into a snarl and practically growl when I say, ". . . And they took him out and they shot him."

"That's great, that's great," he says, "but your hands . . ."

"My hands?"

"Make them fists. Like you want to punch someone."

I do.

I plot my journey to the audition carefully so there is no getting lost and on the day I still give myself plenty of time. Climbing up out of the subway darkness and into the light of Forty-Second Street I absorb energy and purpose all around and want to latch on to it. People walk—no, they step, they march, they stride to where they want to go. At Forty-Sixth Street a statue attracts my attention and I see that it's George M. Cohan and I remember how much I loved *Yankee Doodle Dandy,* the movie about him starring James Cagney.

Cagney was so tough he could tap dance and not look silly. I recite lines from the movie in my head: "My father thanks you, my mother thanks you, my sister thanks you, and I thank you!" It doesn't matter to me that the real man and the actor are blended in my mind; I'm glad to be standing where something big happened.

I walk uptown some more and notice that lots of stores have GOING OUT OF BUSINESS SALE signs plastered all over them and I'm attracted to the ones selling "real Irish lace." I think I should buy Ma a nice cheap lace tablecloth before it's too late. As I walk on I see a picture of an actress outside of a theater that I know is not a movie house. She has a tattoo of a heart on her shoulder, short hair, and a cute, tough look on her face. *Is that a real person?* I wonder. Is she in that theater dancing around like James Cagney did in *Yankee Doodle Dandy,* every night?

Right next door to the theater is a nightclub—I think—I can't be sure because the windows are painted black. A man comes out in a tight paisley shirt, wearing gold chains, and hands out flyers of sexy girls as he invites anybody to come in and see them and even get a free drink. I can tell by the clock up in the sky on a big building that I have time to walk around some more so I find myself in front of Manny's Music looking at all the congas and maracas and wondering if Tito Puente went shopping for timbales there. Right there, right in front of me, he might have walked! I keep going and suddenly find myself in a different world. This is one of Jewish people—not the downtown world of knishes but a world of diamonds and jewels! Store window after store window is full of glittering things.

There is so much of everything around here, lace tablecloths in going-out-of-business stores, congas and maracas at Manny's Music, and now diamonds everywhere. So many things I am tempted to look around even more when I realize it's time to audition. I have to run, I'm not sure where I am—but suddenly I'm there, right in front of the school! Neighborhoods can be as big as a street around here, so you can go from one world to another in seconds.

The High School of Performing Arts has a stone facade and a huge, red, arched door. Inside it smells like minestrone soup. Monitors help me find the audition room along a dark hallway with a linoleum floor and institutional green wainscoting. It reminds me of the old part of P.S. 4 when I lived on Third Avenue. There are other kids—white ones, black ones, but no Puerto Rican ones that I can see. Everybody looks nervous—some even have their mothers with them. We eye one another, but all I can think of are the GOING OUT OF BUSINESS SALE signs and how, if I want to buy nice napkins for Ma, I should do it quickly. Will they have gone out of business by the time I finish my audition?

I take my seat and wait, thinking about what a great neighborhood, or bunch of neighborhoods, this is and how I would never get bored if I went to school here.

A girl comes out of the audition. Her mother looks at her expectantly. They meet and whisper urgently and I hear them say they'll get a bite to eat and talk about it. The girl looks like she is going to pass out as her mother holds her hand and wipes her brow. What a chicken. There's nothing to be afraid of here. A banging door in the night and a wild-eyed father—that's something to be afraid of, not this.

When it's my turn I think about my mother's advice when things get tough: "Close your eyes and keep on going." I enter a regular classroom with chairs pushed against the wall. There are a few teachers but I only notice a tiny one dressed all in black with big jewelry and fluffy black hair, because she is so pretty. We say hello, blah,

blah, blah . . . and I finally sit down and go into my monologue and do everything like I've practiced. Squishing up my face and bunching up my fists like the teacher told me to. Then they tell me to wait. Outside I think about whether or not somebody ever took *me* out to lunch like that girl was being taken. Yes, I have been taken out to lunch a few times, but it wasn't to make me feel better, it was just to eat. And then there was the time Bon Bon was in the hospital for a few days and Uncle Eddie took his son, Little Eddie, and me to eat at a diner three nights straight, but I also remember Ma taking me to the last Automat in the city before it closed down. We put a nickel in a slot and got a piece of apple pie . . .

Then they call me back in. The pretty little one speaks with a melody in her voice: "Do you know what an improvisation is?"

"No."

"Acting without a script. Making it up as you go along."

"Like making believe?"

"Yes," she goes on. "Make believe you are outside a movie theater waiting for a friend who is late."

I make believe I'm waiting for my sister outside of the Fenway and entertain myself by finding a tissue in my pocket, tossing it up, and keeping it in the air until my sister gets there. I am lost in the tissue when the teacher stops me.

"Ever go to the theater?"

"No, but I heard it on a record."

"What did you hear?"

I know this will surprise and impress them because they will not expect a Puerto Rican from the Bronx to say:

"I like *Hamlet*—on the record."

She perks up. Stirs a bit. I think I got her.

"What do you mean?" she asks.

"My sister has a recording of *Hamlet* by Richard Burton."

Again they stir. Silly, really, the whole world knows who Richard Burton is. But I am lucky they can't believe *I* know who he is.

"What did you think?"

"I think I liked Richard Burton's voice. Like I could almost see the spit coming out of his mouth. I bet people got spit on if they sat close, or even the other actors—I'm sure Richard Burton spit on one of them."

"Anything else?"

"I think that if he can make me feel so much on a record, it must really be great to see him in person." I'm not lying. He does make me feel sorry for Hamlet sometimes, but I don't tell them about long, boring parts of the record that put me to sleep, knowing that isn't what they want to hear.

On my way home, as I step down into the subway, I am sorry that I have to leave the light and sparkle and excitement of Forty-Second Street to go back, back, back into the dull darkness of the Bronx.

Weeks later I find out that I have been accepted.

My sister and her friends are very happy for me. "We knew you'd get in," they all say. Ma is happy, too.

"You got in?"

"Yep!"

"You go, go, go, baby!"

I am glad Ma wants me to go, even though I can tell she has no real idea about where I'm going. And I am happy, too—and all I can think of is that now I will be able to leave the Bronx every day and come up in the light of day in Manhattan and that I should buy Ma a lace tablecloth from one of the stores that is going out of business!

PART 3
The Beginning

CHAPTER 1

Performing Arts

We are spread all over. My friend Rita goes to Central Commercial High; Vanessa goes into a special ed class in the local high school because she thinks it's fun to pull the emergency cord on the subway when there is no emergency.

"Why do you do things like that, Vanessa?" I ask her.

"Because my friends dare me to," she reasons, laughing.

And I can't help laughing along with her.

Yvonne runs away with the farting boyfriend, and Lisa and Dolores recede into my past double-time as I take the number six train to the High School of Performing Arts and my Bronx slips away one train station at a time as I fly to planet PA.

Getting off at Forty-Second Street and Grand Central Station, taking the shuttle to Times Square and walking to Forty-Sixth Street, I notice the GOING OUT OF BUSINESS signs are *still* on display though months have passed since I first saw them. Seems to me they would've been out of business by now. There are so many kids smoking outside the school, with some girls sucking in the smoke so deliberately their mouths form square chutes, I think it's really the Professional Smokers School I'm going to.

Musicians stumble around with instruments and sheets of music jammed and wadded into their briefcases, but the dance students really stand out. Ballet dancers are thin and float around on duck feet, while the modern dancers live closer to the ground with concave stomachs and thick feet encased in wooden clogs. All the dancers have long hair they wear naturally—be it straight, curly, or frizzy. There is one Puerto Rican dancer boy from the Bronx who is so happy to be a student there he practically floats on pointe all the time. We are all happy to be here and wonder who will remain because we've been told over and over again that we are all on probation and can be thrown out any minute. The threat of being banished to our neighborhood schools hangs over all of us like smog.

Almost immediately I get sucked into the swirling vortex of smart-ass kids who make outrageous statements. There are two Vanessas in our homeroom. "Which one is Vanessa Washington?" someone asks. "Who do you think?" answers a boy named Melvin. "The black one, with a name like *Washington*!" And I think, *Washington is a black name?* But Melvin should know; he himself is as black as can be. He is always writing in a spiral notebook, and when I find out he's writing poetry I can barely keep my eyes off him and his slim waist and the way he dresses in jackets and pants of corduroy and brown boots.

I even hear shocking talk in the bathroom.

"I've got to cram a tam." A goofy-looking girl grins at me as we adjust our hair in the mirror.

I thought virgins couldn't use those things. But I say nothing— just look on dumbly as she grins at me one last time before going into the stall just as another girl comes into the bathroom carrying a viola.

"Is that you, Holly?" the tampon crammer asks.

"Yeah."

"Are you coming into the city this weekend?"

"You bet—anything to get out of Brooklyn," replies Viola Girl.

What city are they talking about? New York? I thought Brooklyn *was* part of New York City. Why do they call Manhattan "the city"? When they head out together I hear them say "masturbate" before breaking into giggles and I don't know what's so funny because I don't know what that word means, and I have to repeat it— *masturbate, masturbate, masturbate,* over and over again in my head so I can write it down and look it up later. Rushing into Spanish class, I scribble it on my notebook, *m-a-s-t* . . . , but before I'm done more sharp and clever kids spiral around me. One sings:

The sun shines east
The sun shines west
The sun shines north
But my mother does it best!
I got the Oedipus blues.

And everybody in the room laughs. What is that song about? "My mother does it best?" Does what best? What I'm *thinking*— something that has to do with sex?

"Atención, estudiantes. ¡Pongan atención en sus tareas!"

It's the teacher, Miss Bruzio, who is pretty and wears red tights and conducts the whole class in Spanish and I understand all that she is saying. In the Bronx all the kids born in Puerto Rico knew much more Spanish than I did, but here I think I can rule.

"¿Quién fue el gran liberador de Suramérica?" asks Miss Bruzio.

"How should I know who the liberator of South America was?" quips a girl. "Zorro?"

I suppress a laugh as I get ready for Miss Bruzio to yell and scold and discipline but the opposite happens. She laughs along with everyone before moving on to the next topic.

In English class there is a red-haired girl who is not into fun and games and joking around. She was in a fire and has scars on her face and arms and is always so boiling mad I wonder if she didn't cause the fire herself through internal spontaneous combustion. She writes a poem called "The Cloak" and reads it to the class. "'Are the challenges I take like a cloak too big? Are they too big for me to hold up around the shoulders, and so long as to trip me up?'"

Someone coughs. Fire Girl stops reading.

"Continue," says the teacher. He doesn't wear red tights like the Spanish teacher but has the habit of absentmindedly stretching a rubber band around his glasses while listening. Fire Girl shrugs and sits down.

"No," she says. "I don't want to read it anymore. People aren't listening," and she folds up the precious paper and puts it away safe from everyone. I look to see if the teacher will yell and call her fresh and say, "Just who do you think you are?" but he doesn't. He actually looks embarrassed and practically snaps the rubber band right onto his own nose.

Lunch gives me time to regroup and think and ponder and watch as I eat my tuna-fish sandwich from home in the main locker room/lobby/acting class area that throbs with music as we eat with the entire student body dancing all around me like we're on *American Bandstand* on television, only these kids throw in some pirouettes. After lunch I remain in the lobby for class. The acting teacher explains an assignment. (She is not like Miss Pellman—this one doesn't notice me at all.) We are to find a personal prop and manipulate it as if we were alone with no one watching. Over the next few days we sit in a semicircle, performing and observing. It's Fire Girl's turn. We watch her write in a notebook. The teacher is not satisfied.

"Is there something else you might do that is private?"

"My poetry is very private," she says.

But the teacher wants more. "Do you ever put on makeup?" she presses.

Fire Girl seems to diminish. "Well . . ."

"Let's do this," the teacher continues. "Let's make believe you are putting on makeup to go to a dance."

Fire Girl begins to apply imaginary cream to her face. Her hand begins to shake. Suddenly tremors roll through her body, ending in quiet streams of tears. The teacher, alarmed, hands her a tissue but Fire Girl stands up, walks to her locker, collects her things, and waltzes out the door. We never see her again. The school didn't throw her out—she threw the school out.

My turn. I decide to make believe I am making my brother a sandwich, like I used to do before heading out to Crotona Park. Putting my hair in a ponytail, though it's not my best look, and wearing a kid's white T-shirt, though my breasts strain against it, I begin, when the teacher stops me.

"I don't know what you are doing."

I freeze even as I feel heat flooding my face and hear blood rushing around my head.

"And in that T-shirt . . . ? I don't know . . . what you even look like. Are you trying to be some frontierswoman?"

I am so lost I can barely fumble back to my seat. Another girl gets up and her private moment is sorting though her grandmother's jewelry. She picks up a brooch, feels its weight, and holds it to her heart.

"Very good," says the teacher, excited. "You loved your grandmother very much, didn't you?"

Alarmed that I didn't catch that myself, I wonder if I will ever be able to perform that way.

Finally, at the end of that round of exercises, the teacher says, "I want you all to go home and write an essay about your hopes and dreams." This is what I write:

My mother's childhood during the Depression in Puerto Rico makes Oliver Twist's childhood sound nice. My mother told me many sad stories about how poor she was in Puerto Rico. So she came to this country, but she's poor here, too. Still we are really, really, poor. I have an older sister and two younger brothers. One has asthma and my parents sent him to the very place they suffered the most. Some people think home is a good place no matter what. Not me. My father drinks and beats up my mother every chance he gets. I wish my parents would get a divorce so I can come from a broken home—these are my hopes and dreams.

The next day the teacher notices me and involuntarily seeks me out with each glance she gives the whole group. I am happy to be noticed but sorry that it is because of my life at home and not because of *me*.

CHAPTER 2

Winner or Loser?

Over the next couple of weeks I watch out for kids with red-rimmed eyes because they would've been put on probation, and I am shocked when I see Puerto Rican Dancer Boy from the Bronx weeping in the hallway. He does not turn away from me when I see him, as if he is just as shocked as I am about what is happening.

At least he knows why he cries. My own tears are always below the surface and float up when I least expect them to: reading a passage about the Civil War in English class, losing a pencil, singing a song in class with Chute Smoker.

"Are you okay?" Chute Smoker asks me later outside as she expertly turns away from the wind to light her cigarette.

"Yeah, yeah . . ."

She looks at me as she blows smoke out of the side of her mouth and doesn't say anything else and I think that's why I like her.

"Listen, can you come over and babysit my brother, the little jerk, Sunday night? I have to go somewhere with my parents. My mom will pay you."

"Well . . ."

"Come on, say yes. It'll be easy. He'll probably fall asleep early anyway, he's such a jerk. It'll be easy money."

"Well . . ."

"Come on," she urges, sucking up her smoke.

On Sunday I go to her address on West End Avenue and Eighty-Sixth Street and am surprised I can't tell what kind of neighborhood I am in because there is a little bit of everything—white, black, Jewish, Puerto Rican. I'm really impressed that her building has a doorman and even more impressed when the elevator opens on a floor that only has one door. Hers!

"Hey," she says, grinning when she sees me.

Her apartment is a museum, or a library, or a church, or some-place that has floor-to-ceiling bookcases, and paintings on the walls, and African masks that look for real. They have a whole wall of long-playing albums and a speaker system with two big speakers facing an L-shaped leather sofa. The music I hear is a cool and jazzy trumpet. Chute Smoker's parents have longish hair—the mother wears a necklace of great huge coral beads; the father peers at me through big black-framed glasses.

"Hi there," they say in unison, taking my coat. Their eyes can't help flicking over me and I realize I am overdressed in a skirt and stockings and they are wearing blue jeans. Smiling back like a fool I ask where the bathroom is. It's a splash of color with red, green, blue, and yellow towels all draped neatly over the racks. Opposite the toilet at eye level is a chart (I figure) of French verbs and their conjugations. I rinse my hands but don't know if it's okay to use one of the towels so I flick my fingers around and dry my hands on my skirt.

"Everything come out all right?" asks her little brother.

He has a cold and sits on the sofa with a red nose and an angry look on his face.

"Don't be a little jerk," says my friend.

"Enough," says her mother. "Let's go." Then to me, "We won't be back late—just out to The French Institute for a lecture on Paris during World War Two."

"We're all going this summer," says her dad, helping her mother on with her coat. I can't imagine my father helping my mother on with her coat.

As soon as they leave, the little boy commands me, "Put on the television, will you?" I am at a loss because I am figuring I have to turn off the music first. Reading my mind, he says, pointing, "Just hit that switch over there." I follow orders then stand at attention, waiting for his next command. "Now turn the television on!"

As we watch I am struck with drowsiness and cannot keep my eyes open. When I momentarily nod off, he scolds me sharply, "Hey, you're not supposed to fall asleep, you know!" And I feel like I'm the little kid and he is the older one. Thankfully, next on TV is *The Ed Sullivan Show*. The Temptations are on and I love their close harmonies and the smooth moves they make to accentuate the lyrics of the song. But the little boy sneers, "Why do they have to do all those dance moves when they sing?" as if the performers disgust him with the ridiculousness of their steps. I am embarrassed that I don't have an answer and that this little kid has made me feel dumb. When my friend and her parents return I am anxious to leave. "Wait," says Chute Smoker. "I'll walk you to the train."

Once outside she confides in me. "I just wanted to get out for a smoke! Listen—next Saturday I have the place all to myself. I'm having a sleepover party. Can you come?"

"No . . . I . . ."

"Oh come on, it'll be fun."

"I don't know . . ." I say, grasping around for an excuse. "I can't sleep over," I finally blurt out. "I have to take care of my little brother . . . give him breakfast."

"What? How old is he anyway?"

"Eight."

"So—can't he pour his own Cheerios?"

I duck down into the train station so I don't have to answer.

The teacher announces she is going to cast us in roles that are similar to our personalities, and I'm embarrassed I'm cast as the drab, shy character Amy in the play *One Sunday Afternoon*. Is that how she sees me? As the dreary one? The part of the beautiful, flirty, vivacious character Virginia goes to my scene partner, Mariel, who is a vision in beige, with champagne-blonde satiny hair that hangs to her shoulders, and white, beige, or gray soft turtleneck sweaters, and wool miniskirts. I compare her look to mine. Watching Miss Kitty on *Gunsmoke* inspired Vanessa to make me an outfit, so I'm wearing a purple blouse and matching purple garter and I feel like I'm wearing a costume while Mariel wears real clothes. We are supposed to practice our scenes, but I can't stop looking at Mariel's tiny feet encased in soft, caramel-colored leather boots. She sees me looking, so, trying to tuck my big feet under the chair, I say, "I like your boots."

"Oh God, I know, thank you, I like these boots, too, I got them at Bendel's. God, I didn't think I'd ever be able to wear shoes again much less boots! You'll never guess what happened to me last summer. I was on my boyfriend's motorcycle and we were charging around Main Street in East Hampton and the bike didn't have a muffler on it and we saw a cop car and you'll never guess what I did. Oh my God, I tried to stick my toe in the exhaust pipe so it wouldn't make any noise and I burned it! I had to wear a bandage on my toe for a week!"

We spot the teacher coming our way. "Shhh . . . here she comes!" And we start practicing our scene about two turn-of-the-century girls waiting for blind dates.

"What happened?" is the teacher's only remark when we finally perform.

"I thought my own nervousness would come through as the *character's* nervousness," I say lamely.

Her face falls. Then she says, "You have no energy, Sonia. You must go to the theater, Sonia, so you can see how actresses move."

Is she kidding? Go to the theater? I don't have any money to go to the theater. And even if I did I wouldn't know what to see. But I can practice having energy, so at home on Saturday I make myself fried eggs and greasy bacon sandwiches. That'll give me the boost I need!

"Get out of the house while I set off a roach bomb," says Ma. "Stay out as long as you can so the smell don't make Joe sick."

I eat, then Joe and Petey and I escape while Ma's on her roach warpath. Walking ahead or behind my brothers I practice being peppy and just bursting with vitality. But hours later when we get home Joe gets sick anyway. Ma stops sweeping up the roaches and sits with him at the window. His stomach almost touches the back of his spine as he tries to suck in air. I'm skipping around the apartment on roach detail, sweeping them up and tossing them into the trash, when my father comes home.

"What the hell!" he sputters, in a rage that Joe is sick.

Joe breathes in deeper. Ma goes to my father.

"*¡Cálmate!*"

But he will not be calmed. He lashes out, shouting that he would like to grab God by the neck and strangle Him for giving us such bad luck. I do jumping jacks as they talk about taking Joe to Lincoln Hospital again—this is the third time this week Joe's gotten sick, with Ma calming Pops as he rages. Or is it Pops raging, Joe getting sick, Ma calming? Whichever order of events it is, Joe's attacks have more energy than any mojo I can come up with.

Things start out the same way the next year.

"What animal should I be?" I ask the teacher. This teacher is the young and pretty one who auditioned me. She is still very tiny, dressed in black and large pieces of silver jewelry, with caramel lipstick as the only hint of color.

"Any animal with energy," she sighs. "How about a rabbit?"

"Yes, okay, a rabbit." We are to make our own costumes. I tell the pretty teacher I'll make my costume purple and green.

"Hmm . . . how about soft pink and yellow?" she says, and I know she is alluding to my garish taste.

So I go to the Central Park Zoo and examine the behavior of a rabbit but all it does is squint. I squint in class and the teacher throws her hands up in despair because I didn't hippity-hop.

At home, Ma is cleaning and singing ". . . *in the still of the niiight . . .*" when I complain to her. "How are you at playing humans?" she jokes, going back to her song. I feel tired and don't know if I'll ever be good at playing humans and even wonder if I really want to be an actress.

But my thinking changes after seeing a senior actor whose performance is so wonderful I am swept into the story going on, on the stage. Suddenly I want to be able to do that as well and I get a chance to try when I am assigned a scene from a play called *Street Scene*. Not only that—my scene partner is the school's beloved romantic poet, Melvin. I play the daughter of an Irish drunk who accidentally kills his wife. We sit down with the teacher, and I start out feeling calm and fine reading make-believe lines about why the murder happened. Words that say people shouldn't depend on each other for everything. Not stuff like food or furniture but things we need inside our hearts or some such stuff like that and really, to tell you the truth, I don't even know what all that stuff means. Except I wonder, even as I'm reading, if it's things like love or loneliness? Like if we don't feel loved we shouldn't expect someone else to love us? Or if we're lonely we can't expect someone else to make us feel better by hanging out with us. That we should know how to love ourselves, and hang out with ourselves somehow. But really, I think again, I don't know what all the words in this play mean but in the middle of that thought, which is in the middle of that speech, I am hit with an emotion so strong and unexpected it's like the smack of a rifle butt on the back of my head and I start to blubber. Embarrassed at my sudden incoherent, out-of-control behavior Melvin looks at his boots and the teacher regards me as I try to pull myself together. Every character in this play is like someone I know.

"Maybe this isn't the right time for you to work on this scene," she says carefully, as if talking to a lunatic.

"Why not? It's perfect for me," I answer. I can't believe it! First I don't have energy and now I'm too emotional.

"Perhaps you can't handle it at this stage of your life," she adds soothingly. "Let's look at some other scene for you to work on," she adds.

Once again I'm thrown off course.

CHAPTER 3

What Skin Am I In?

I wish I knew how it would feel to be free . . ."

That summer I find myself singing at the top of my lungs with a group called the Urban Arts Corps. It's a job I got through the school to bring theater to kids in poor neighborhoods, and I love it, but what I love even more is this song, though my heart breaks and my tears come every time we sing it.

I look around at my fellow singers in the rehearsal hall: Some are students from Performing Arts like me, some are our alumni, some are young actors from Harlem, and some performers are even from the South. Our leader is Vinnette Carroll, a great big woman with a booming voice, who has come to Performing Arts to teach. She watches us with tiny, twinkly eyes made even smaller by her thick glasses, in her man sandals and shapeless dress, still looking cute because of her bemused smile and hair worn in a childish pouf on her head. I liked her even before I learned she is a magician who makes theater out of thin air. We read a story called "The Lottery" about small-town folk who ritualistically stone one of their own. In the climactic moment the poor victim fights for her life, screaming, "It isn't fair, it isn't right!" as we mime bashing her head in. In Miss Carroll's hands, those screams have something to do with civil rights.

We perform a skit that requires white people, so what do we do when there are no white people in the group? We make signs that read HONKY or CRACKER and have the white characters wear them. It makes me laugh as hard as I did when Vanessa and I discussed our purple gums. It still feels good to look something scary in the face and laugh.

Still, the best part of this job is the music. When we get to sing, "... *I wish you could know what it means to be me* ..." I don't know why I cry, but I do.

That September Melvin makes the first move by inviting me to his house. But I'm too nervous to go alone so I bring Vanessa. I don't wear purple blouses and garters anymore—I'm into wearing Indian saris since Bill, now my sister's husband, has become a merchant seaman and he brought me one from Calcutta.

"How do I look, Vanessa?"

"Like an *idiota*," she laughs.

And I laugh along with her but I wear it anyway.

Melvin lives in the East Ninety-Sixth Street projects. We walk in and have to get past his mother, who is in the kitchen cooking.

"Hi, Mrs. Hall."

"Hello—he's in the back."

We go past her normal-looking living room with a picture of Martin Luther King, Jr., and Kennedy on the television set into the other world of Melvin's hippie room, and I'm glad Vanessa is with me because Melvin's best friend, Oscar Rodriguez, and a ballerina are there, too. Is it a party? The room is fragrant with incense. There are posters of Bob Dylan and Richie Havens and Jimi Hendrix. Melvin's bedspread has an Indian paisley print on it, and I think I match it perfectly in my sari. Melvin is so beautiful with his dark,

dark skin and his slim hips in tight corduroy pants. His spiral poetry notebook is as worn and used as Don Joe's credit/debit composition notebook back on Third Avenue. Melvin sits on his bed; his jacket is thrown on a chair, his brown boots peek out from under the bedspread. He is so cool he can say hello to us in his stocking feet. Oscar Rodriguez strums on a guitar. Vanessa pulls out a joint.

"Okay . . ." says Melvin. Now we are getting somewhere.

We smoke it. Melvin reads a poem about the universe or something.

"Wow . . ." I say dreamily. "I love it." But I don't really know what he is talking about. Vanessa giggles. Oscar plays his guitar then invites Vanessa to go for a walk. She giggles as they leave. Melvin reads some famous poet I never heard of—like I have ever heard of *any* poet—and I make believe I'm listening but I'm really fantasizing about what perfect couples we make. I see us—me and Melvin and Vanessa and Oscar—going on dates to the zoo, with Oscar holding hands with Vanessa and me holding hands with Melvin, then coming back and listening to Simon and Garfunkel. Then, when Vanessa and I get our own apartment, they can come over for dinner.

The next day at school I ask Oscar what he thought of her.

"She's stupid," he says.

"No she isn't!" I am furious. "She just doesn't speak English!"

"No," he answers. "I was speaking Spanish with her. She's stupid."

"You didn't mind smoking her joint."

"What does that have to do with anything, Sonia?"

"You think you're so hip. Well, she's hipper."

Two days later she comes over to my house with a joint. We smoke it. A Beatles song drifts through my brain so I sing, ". . . *I am the walrus . . . I am the walrus . . .*" Vanessa grins at me. "Hey, Vanessa, what do you think that song means?"

"*¿Qué?*" She starts giggling.

"You know—that Beatles song . . . *I am the walrus . . .* what do you think it means?"

"*¿Qué se yo?* How should I know?" she says.

I go on, "You know, Vanessa, as soon as we graduate we can get jobs as secretaries. What do you think?"

"*Sí, sí . . .*"

She pulls out a bag of cookies. "*¿Quieres?*"

"Sure," I say, stuffing my mouth. "Will your mother have any trouble letting you move out?"

"*¿Ah?*" she laughs.

"Your mother . . ."

"Let's go make *a dress for you to wear* tomorrow!" she says, pulling me out of the apartment.

I decide to fall in love with someone else. He is an underclassman. His parents have an apartment in a luxury high-rise on Fourteenth Street and are never home. I visit him for long days on weekends in my new look: hip beatnik. Black turtleneck sweaters, pointy black suede shoes with a low heel and a Pilgrim buckle, black tights, and a plaid skirt. My hair is parted in the middle and I pull it back into a tight bun like a ballerina.

"If my parents died today," he says after we roll around on his bed for an hour or two, "all this would be mine. Just imagine, it could happen, their plane could be crashing right now and I would inherit this co-op."

I look out the window on to the neighborhood. We are on the west side of Fourteenth Street, but I know if you go to the east side of Fourteenth it will be a whole different story, with Puerto Rican restaurants galore that serve the kinds of food my father likes, *cuchifritos,* pigs' ears and tongues, and blood sausage called *morcilla.* It's the kind of food that turns Ma's stomach whenever he brings it home. Mine, too, really.

"Come," says my boyfriend, pulling me away from the window and onto the bed again to continue his fantasy of home ownership. "All this could be mine!" After a day spent making believe he is independently wealthy I make my way home on the subway.

The next time we meet he takes me to a restaurant called Serendipity. It's famous and beautiful and expensive, and I am thrilled that we come across a classmate dining with her whole family. She eyes me enviously as I sit with a date and she is stuck with her mom, dad, and bratty little sister.

One day at school he invites me to a party. All that week I work on a special dress because I want to look good. It's lime green with a square neckline and bell sleeves and I wear it with white fishnets and beige shoes. When I get to his apartment he is wearing gray pants, a cream turtleneck pullover, and a double-breasted blue blazer with brass buttons. I am excited about the party but shocked when we get there. It is all boys. And they are all prettier than me. They all have long bangs they flip around, and sweep off their brows with their delicate middle fingers. They point and giggle that their friend has brought a girl with him.

"Who is your friend?" says one seductively.

"This is Sonia . . ." says my boyfriend sheepishly.

We dance and I can't believe all the boys dance with each other and I think I see some of them kissing. I have never even read about stuff like that!

We are quiet on our way to the subway where I will go uptown and he will go down. I don't know words to ask the question on my mind.

The next time we meet I decide to take him to a restaurant on Fourteenth Street and plan it out carefully.

"I want to show you part of my culture," I say coyly, dragging him east toward the Puerto Rican section of Fourteenth Street, where we can have our choice of *cuchifrito* joints. San Juan Cuchifritos, Dos Hermanos Cuchifritos, Cuchifritos del Caribe. I pick the one with the grimiest window and most flies dancing around the bare bulbs warming pigskin cracklings on display.

"Come on in. We eat this stuff all the time at my house," I lie.

I order pigs' ears and tongue and black blood sausage. When the food comes he looks like he might throw up and I feel triumphant at his look of distaste. I'm proud that I am tougher than he is, and prove it by stuffing my face. But later when I am alone on the train home, my victory doesn't taste so good at all. Plus—my stomach is turning and *I'm* the one who feels like throwing up.

The next day I wear the outfit Vanessa and I made—a large T-shirt-shaped dress with a handkerchief belt—and I see Puerto Rican Dancer Boy from the Bronx standing around outside the school. He's dyed his curly black hair white-blond and he looks like he is trying to peer into the school through the bricks with his wild red-rimmed eyes, he wants in so badly. Before he disappears altogether I see him outside the school now and again like he has nowhere else to go, and I wonder how come he is out and not me?

CHAPTER 4

The Love and Marriage Bomb

The gown I'm wearing is white and slim with a green sash at the waist, and when I look up from the seamstress fussing around the hem I am shocked at the Sonias staring back at me from a three-way mirror because they are beautiful; I'm embarrassed to feel that way about myself. My hair cascades down and I am surprised at how grown up I look, though I'm not yet, really—only fifteen. At eighteen my cousin Carmen is the real woman ready to be married, and through the whole preparation for the wedding I feel that I have my nose pressed up against the future that I hope will be mine. We have been getting ready every weekend for the past month. Ma is in the lead for three reasons: She is the maid of honor, she can navigate around the Italian dress shop ladies because these are the kind of women she works with, and she's the only one who drives. Uncle Eddie has some big part in it as well. I am a bridesmaid along with whatever friends Carmen has left who haven't been "wronged" yet.

On the wedding day we all dress in Carmen's house on Elder Avenue. It's crammed with so much Italian-style mirrors and plastic-covered furniture I think there must be a water fountain with cement babies spouting water somewhere in the kitchen. Carmen insists we all wear a beehive hairdo or big fat curls piled on top of our heads and has asked a few of her friends to come over and beat and tease our hair into shape. I hate my hairdo, remembering how much better I looked with it falling down around my shoulders, and it makes me feel even more self-conscious when I meet my wedding partner. But no matter—all the bridesmaids' partners are in their twenties and interested in the older girls. Carmen is demure and shy and sacrificial and I study her so I can be the same way when it's my turn to get married.

It's the perfect wedding. No basement Puerto Rican social club serving rice and beans and greasy pork shoulders with green bananas for us—we go to Sorrento's, the fancy Italian party rental space that serves chicken in white sauce. Knowing my partner thinks I'm a kid, I decide to make my partner laugh by speaking with an exaggerated Puerto Rican accent.

"Joo like eet een dees place?" I think I'm hilarious, but Ma shoots me a look that tells me to knock it off, so I watch my uncles' suspicious looks at the chicken dish served floating around milky white sauce, as pure as Carmen herself. I know she is untouched because she passed Manny's virgin test.

"How did you test her?" I had asked.

"Well, I tried to have sex with her—telling her that we might as well—after all, we were getting married."

"And what happened?"

"She hit me."

"She hit you!"

"Well, yeah—not hard but still a slap—that's when I knew she was the woman for me."

"What if she had gone 'all the way'?" I remembered that term from *True Confessions* magazines.

He looks at me like the answer is so obvious he can't believe I'm asking.

"What do you think? I wouldn't have married her."

Six months later I am standing on the landing of a semiattached house at the edge of the earth. There are wild animal sounds and huge birds I come to know as egrets flying all around. Somehow my mother has managed to put a down payment on a brand-new home in a new development in the upper Bronx. It's so in the middle of nowhere you have to take two buses, a train, and then walk an additional five blocks to get to it.

The house has stairs leading up to three bedrooms, just like houses on television that actresses sweep down on! I feel like I'm making a grand entrance each time I go to the kitchen downstairs. My parents take the largest room, my brothers share another, and I get my own. No more sharing rooms with brothers I don't like that much. Privacy at last. I don't know how Ma did it, but she was probably inspired by Uncles Eddie and Frank, who had already moved up in the world by buying houses. The day we move in Bon Bon sprinkles sugar in all the kitchen cabinets and drawers for good luck.

But something goes wrong with us almost immediately. Right after dinner, on the very day we move in, when Ma wants to sit and enjoy her stupendous accomplishment, my father dresses to go out.

"Where are you going?" Ma asks.

"I'll be back soon," he answers.

And the look on her face is so full of disappointment I have to look away, to give her privacy. Later she sits outside on the tiny cement landing and stares at the sky, looking for answers, and I am bewildered as well that a house didn't make us live happily ever after.

The next day the kitchen drawers and cabinets are crawling with ants eating Bon Bon's good-luck sugar sprinkling.

Ma gets rid of the ants in time for my sweet sixteenth birthday. I ask some old friends from Southern Boulevard, and some new ones from Performing Arts. The morning of the party I set my hair in curlers and polish my nails. When my nails and hair are perfectly done, I put on my bridesmaid gown from Carmen's wedding and sweep down the stairs to greet my uncle Eddie, who gives me a hug, a kiss, and sixteen roses before going into the kitchen to drink coffee with Ma. As I wait for guests to arrive, I work on my *señorita* performance of being the ripe prize the world is dying to pluck.

I have never acted better. My smile radiantly shines through me as I look out the window into the distance. Not since Juliet waited for Romeo is waiting so beautifully done, and I sustain this performance even after hours have passed and it is clear to me that no one is coming. Not even Vanessa.

I take off my dress and join Ma on the landing of our steps outside.

"So, Vanessa, where the fuck were you?"

It's a week later and I'm standing just inside a storefront on West Farms Road, now made into a makeshift apartment. Vanessa doesn't answer and I add, "What are you, a Gypsy?"

Vanessa shoves me the way she used to but we don't burst into laughter as quickly anymore—there is sourness behind her perfect cheeks. "Shhh . . ." she says, indicating her mother in the back room. The front windows are covered with black curtains. (I think the Gypsies used red.) There is a dresser inside the door and a double bed just a few steps in. Past that there is a kitchen and a cot. I wonder what happened to the white-and-gold Louis XIV furniture that was stuffed in the Southern Boulevard apartment. Her mother enters from the back with the biggest, meanest Mexican-looking dude I have ever seen, exactly like the *pistoleros* in the Mexican revolution movies Ma used to take me to. He has thick, wavy hair, a drooping mustache, and wears burgundy cowboy boots with red stitching! I look at Vanessa's blank face.

"You like it?" says her mother, Irena, sprinkling perfume on her soft black coat tossed on the bed. She is getting ready to step out with her man, who impatiently eyes us.

"Take care, Mama," says her mother, kissing Vanessa on the lips. Vanessa's mother calls her "Mama," which I have always thought is weird. Then, carelessly tossing on her big coat and latching on to her big man's arm, she steps out the door. Vanessa smiles at me weakly and I feel sorry that she is to be left alone in a store, like something for sale.

But maybe Vanessa wasn't alone too much, because weeks later she joins my sister, her husband, and me for dinner at the house. Ma is stirring the pot when Vanessa drops the bomb!

"What?"

"I'm pregnant . . ."

My sister, Bill, and Ma turn their eyes inward and don't register me no matter how hard I look from one to the other. The blood rushing through my ears cancels out all other noises, but then Vanessa doesn't say much more and just sits there like this is all happening to someone else. I think about all the plans we made. "I thought we were getting an apartment," I say weakly. She still doesn't respond.

Ma gets up and refills our water glasses. My sister cuts into her plantain. Bill seems interested, but only as an audience member, not as a participant.

"There's ways to get out of this," I insist. "You really want to be like my cousin Sue, always having to have someone help you out because you have lots of kids and no money?" And then I immediately think of Carmen and recent images of her ratchet into focus. Pregnant now but who really, I suddenly realize, reminds me of a beautiful bird in a cage looking dazed and disengaged. I turn to my mother for some explanation of this horror but she just gets up again, as if nothing unusual is happening.

"More rice?" she asks the group.

"I'll take some more," says my sister.

Why are they talking about rice? We have to figure a way out of this. This is important. I launch into a monologue.

"Vanessa, it doesn't have to go that way! You're just a kid! You can end this pregnancy. It's the sixties! We are free now." But every argument I throw glances off her expressionless face and disappears into the ozone as she vanishes from within and resignation takes over.

Later, after everyone else has left and Ma has gone out to sit on the cement landing to interpret the sky, I start to hyperventilate. I cannot believe Vanessa would do this! And right then and there I think, *Fuck this, I am out of here.* I will go, go, go as far away as I can from this place where nothing changes.

CHAPTER 5

Oozing Opportunist

I sit in class antsy and bored.

"Ask me my name, ask me my name," the senior acting teacher demands.

"What's your name?" a game student complies.

The teacher states his name, then asks emphatically, "Was I being dismissive, loving, or contradictory?"

"Dismissive," the student offers.

"No, that was loving, loving, loving! I was being loving! Try again, ask me my name."

Oh, who cares, for Christ's sake! I am tired of this relentless acting lesson of guessing games of emotions. And then, after forty minutes of this crap, I have to go play a Jewish maid in a play that takes place in a German girls' boarding school! I think it's funny that all the Jewish girls get to play the Christian German *Fräuleins* and *I* get to play their housekeeper.

"That's how we maintain social balance," says the director cleverly.

Lucky me.

As a cleaning lady I have few lines so I entertain myself in rehearsal by making up a game—when given a command by the *Fräuleins* I open my mouth as if to answer then suddenly press my lips together as if I have changed my mind about answering or they have cut me off. It's funny, and fooling around like that cracks me up every time. I even crack up my Chute Smoker friend until she gets tired of me breaking her concentration and deadpans me into stopping.

Later in class, in a moment when the teacher has stepped out, I pan the room. Melvin is enraptured with a rich, beautiful, red-haired girl with a hook nose who is so perfectly happy with the way she looks I envy her. They thrill each other, recalling the lyrics to the Beatles' "Lucy in the Sky with Diamonds"—convinced the song is about LSD. A few seats from them is the lead girl in the German play. She is going through her lines and the order of the emotions on her face is so clear I know exactly which scene she is working on. I believe that she is the real actress in this bunch, and when a week later the director says that she must cry on cue and she delivers I know my suspicions are correct.

And what about me? What did I do except find everything funny and chase boys I was sure I was smarter than? The teachers of Performing Arts will not recommend me to colleges because my grades are so low and I am too dull an actress, but they have gotten me a job doing clerical work at the American National Theater and Academy—maybe they are preparing me to be a secretary after all. But I won't be a secretary. I'm going to college no matter what.

I become like oozing, moving lava, sliding down a hill, finding and looking to fill every crevice of opportunity, expanding with all of me in every space available before moving on. I don't think, I don't read "how to" flyers and pamphlets on higher education, but I move mindlessly forward to find and fill niches that will hold me. The only possibility for me is to get into college by way of an audition—I will get the money somehow—I just know I will, for how can you stop the flow of things going their natural path? I pick schools in Long Island, Pittsburgh, and one so far upstate New York it's close to Canada, and I walk into my boss's office when I'm ready, to give her the chance to help me.

"I have some . . . college . . . applications . . . and . . . they want . . ."

"Recommendations? Sure, I'll write one for you. No problem."

"Thank you . . ."

"Will the school write you one as well?"

"No . . . they . . ." I don't think I should apologize. It's not my fault I got a crummy education in the Bronx that caused me to be so far behind. So I am honest. "I have terrible grades, so PA won't recommend me to any drama schools."

She takes a moment to think, and before she can change her mind about helping me I make a joke: "I don't know how I could've been so smart in the Bronx and so dumb in Manhattan."

She laughs—I got her on my side. At home I pore over the applications and write the essays telling them all about myself. Martin Luther King, Jr., and the civil rights movement have shifted society to being on my side a little but now it is up to me to step up.

The next thing I have to think about is what to audition with. Why not *Street Scene*? It worked before—why not again? I don't examine it too closely because it might interrupt my moving forward. The day arrives and the auditions are held in a Midtown hotel conference room. I'm wearing a blue sweater that seems cheerful and a black skirt, stockings, and shoes to give me a serious-enough look. Entering the room, I see a few professors seated behind a long table and I focus on one in particular because he has such a precise, nicely organized face and a curious name—Jewel Walker. I take off my shoes to get down to it. Why? I'm not sure except taking off my shoes is like rolling up my sleeves and getting down to work.

As expected, the monologue takes me to another place and I am so overcome with gummy tears I lose my sense of where I am and end up with my back to the professors auditioning me. Blinking rapidly to clear my vision, I find my shoes and put one on.

"Come sit and talk to us . . ." says Jewel Walker.

I turn and limp toward them.

". . . after you put on your other shoe."

Months later I'm filing at ANTA.

"Sonia, step into my office a minute, will you?" My boss smiles coyly. I follow her as she waves me into a chair, picks up a letter from her desk, and teases me with it. "This concerns you, Sonia. Read it."

I do. It's from the head of the Drama Department at Carnegie Mellon University thanking her for the letter of recommendation and saying the school is most happy to accept me. And not only that—they are prepared to give me a scholarship. I'm stunned.

"Congratulations!" she chimes.

I'm stunned.

"It's a great school."

I'm stunned.

"Maybe you'll even like Pittsburgh."

I'm stunned.

"Would you like a glass of water . . . ?"

Aurea was the first to finish high school in our bunch and now I am going to college.

"Thank you, thank you . . ." I croak self-consciously.

"Now, you are not to tell anyone because it's not official yet. Except your family, of course," she adds. "Why don't you take the rest of the afternoon off? Go home and celebrate with them."

When I step out into the daylight I am concerned that my brightness, my glow, might blind some poor unsuspecting people walking up and down Broadway. But people do not stare at me in any way. Still—I find my image in a going-out-of-business store window and I think I *do* look different. Performing Arts will know soon enough, and I don't want to gloat and preen before them; my star aura is too bright for me to stoop so low. I forget about the Performing Arts teachers the minute I see Ma.

"Ma, I got into college!"

"You did!"

"Yes!"

"Which one?"

"Carnegie Mellon."

"What kind of school is it?" she asks.

"Carnegie Mellon University. I'm going for drama."

"Drama?"

"Yeah, like acting."

"Wonderful. What will you learn?"

"I don't know! Theater stuff."

"Like singing?"

"No."

"Okay. Where is it?"

"Pittsburgh."

"Pittsburgh! Why so far?"

"Because they want me."

"But it's so far!"

"And they are going to give me a scholarship."

"A scholarship? *¿Una beca?*"

"*Sí . . .*"

"How come?" Ma wants to know.

I just grin at her.

"Sonia . . ."

"Huh?"

"*¿Qué estás pensando . . . ?*"

"What was I thinking? Oh, nothing . . . just that I'm happy!"

"You go, go, and go, baby!"

CHAPTER 6

Free at Last

Take this bed," Pops suggests, pointing to one near the window. "More fresh air."

Yay! After sticking my head out of the car for five hours, like a dog anxious to get somewhere, we have arrived at my new school in Pittsburgh. Ma and Pops have been in the front seat, stony and silent, and I am glad that Pittsburgh took so long to get to because that means I am really far away from them.

My dorm is a brick building with big pink flowers landscaped all around a circular driveway. The lobby has soft, overstuffed, easy places to sit and talk that can't muffle the undercurrent of excitement. I sign in, run up the stairs, and find my room with Ma and Pops trailing me. Ma bursts into tears the minute I close the door behind us and I ignore her. My father looks uncomfortable, either because of her tears or this fussy place he's in—I can't tell.

They cannot leave soon enough to suit me. I want to be rid of them both, quickly, so I can redefine myself in this place, so after a five-hour trip I hustle them out of the room and into their car as fast as possible. "Bye . . . I'll call you . . . Bye . . ." As soon as they are out of sight I run back to make myself over in this brand-new world. If

I'm really quick and clever I can become whoever I want. Who should I be? I have already been the garter-wearing Kitty from *Gunsmoke* girl, and the sari-wearing East Indian girl, and the solemn intellectual beatnik. What to be now?

I go for the Native American counter-culture look, putting my hair in two long braids, wearing a headband, a sandalwood necklace, and a denim shirt. My new roommate comes in at the middle of my transformation. She is tall, with long, wispy hair a non-color I can't describe. She looks just like all the loafer, kneesock, pleated skirt, and soft-sweater-wearing college girls I've seen in magazines. She holds her hand out and murmurs something I can't hear so I lean in. "Huh?"

She whispers again and I just make it out. "Hello, I'm Sharon. I'm from Columbus, Ohio." Her voice is whispery but I can feel her excitement through her handshake.

"Hi. I'm Sonia from New York City." Sharon's parents come in with boxes of books.

"Hello," they say.

I'm polite and I go through the motions but I can't take my eyes off the books. What are they? Why bring them to school? This is college—don't they have books here already? Has she read them? Will she read them? They unpack and I really don't know what to do so I'm glad when they are done.

"We'll wait downstairs," her parents say.

Sharon smiles at me before following them out the door. "Well, I guess I'll go and walk around with them . . . They want to see me in this great institution of learning . . ."

All of a sudden I want my folks and rush to the window hoping to catch them before they drive away. Don't *I* want them to see me in this great institution of learning, too? But they are gone and I am left wondering.

After one last look in the mirror I go off by myself to see the campus, looking like Pocahontas.

Outside I catch the eye of a very cute blond boy on my way to the drama building, who grins at me. *My God, it's one of the Beach Boys,* I think. I check out the drama building, and when I come out—he's there, still grinning! I have never met a boy so silly and grinning and bold.

"Hey . . ." he says.

"Hey . . ." I say and before the week is over we begin to hang out together all the time, sitting on the school lawn or tossing a Frisbee. He is in a fraternity and wears plaid shirts and loafers. Ha! I'm living the coed life immediately, my old life behind me shed like old skin. *This is going to be a piece of cake,* I think smugly.

But when a week later the teacher who auditioned me, Jewel Walker, invites me over to his house one Sunday for brunch, I am suspicious. Why me? I don't know him. When I get there it's not just me, it's some other kids as well, a blond boy and another girl. We all look at each other and I quickly check them out to see what we have in common, but this isn't the ethnic club or the loser club; we have nothing in common except being in the drama department. Walker serves us oatmeal and bacon! Oatmeal and bacon? What a crazy combination. I eat and wait for a trap to spring.

There is no trap, but when I act, or sing, or even write in class I feel like I am in a hall of mirrors with the ground shifting around under me, not knowing if I'm good or bad, being laughed at or not. Then we are introduced to a big deal visiting professor.

"What's my name? What's my name?" he asks. It's the same teacher I had in high school. Have I come very far at all?

I am a little girl again, and my whole family is sitting around the kitchen table laughing and telling jokes about being really poor in Puerto Rico.

"The baby fell through a hole right in the house . . . !" cackles Aunt Iris. "The river of shit just floated her away . . ."

Everybody laughs.

"And she hadn't eaten in a week," adds Uncle Frank.

This last crack makes everybody double over. I feel nervous and edgy. How is this funny? Then my father, wearing huge, funny-looking boxer shorts, calmly and serenely gets up and goes over to the oven, from which he retrieves a gleaming, hot knife. He sits back down and begins to slice up the thickest part of his thigh. The blood oozing out makes everyone, Uncle Eddie and Uncle Frank and their wives, laugh even harder. I am mesmerized by the color of the blood and how it drips, drips in big drops onto the black-and-white-checkered kitchen floor, when I hear a breathy, whispery voice say, ". . . Sooonnnia."

"Whaaa—?"

"Phone for you."

I wake up, suddenly gasping for air and relieved to see that I am in bed wearing pajamas and in my dorm room and I am eighteen years old and not a little girl in a dream in a Bronx kitchen. Sharon's face comes into focus.

"Phone for you," she repeats.

I look at the clock and see that it's 2:00 a.m., and I stumble out into the brightly lit hallway. Though we've all been in school for months, the girls in the dorm still stay up all night, laughing, talking, doing their nails, and setting their hair. My father is on the line, snarling drunk, complaining about something. I am surprised he is able to dial me and even more shocked that he thought I could help him with whatever was bothering him so many miles away.

"Pops," I say.

He launches into a tirade about something.

"But . . ." He doesn't hear me and goes on. I lean my head against the wall, and place the receiver on my lap until I hear a pause in his monologue that I might be able to break into and say something, but there is no break and I listen until he starts losing steam. I put the phone to my ear.

"Pops!"

"Huh."

"Listen, are you home . . . ?"

"¿Qué?"

"Go to sleep, wherever you are."

He mumbles something and then I hear a click. He's off the phone. Hanging up, I stagger back to bed and hope that I can fall asleep for a long time, and when I finally do a girl's squeal makes me bolt upright on the alert for danger and ready to fight. I stay up and wait for daylight to catch up with me.

Sleepwalking that morning into voice-and-diction class, I sit in the back of the room and watch Sharon recite a Shakespearean sonnet while trying to control her breathy voice.

" 'Shall I compare thee to a summer's day . . .' " she whispers.

"My dear," drawls the teacher. "You must connect with your inner core . . . your . . ."

Sharon stops, shakes her head slightly, and heads out of the class, eyes brimming. I feel bad for her. Back in the room she sits on her bed reading and I wonder what it is, and if it will make her feel better.

"I hate that class, too," I say.

Sharon whispers a self-conscious laugh. "No matter what I do . . . I can't seem to please that professor . . ."

"Who wants to talk like that anyway?" I add. For a moment she and I have things in common. "Thanks for getting me up for the phone last night."

She closes the book after carefully putting in a bookmark. "You're welcome," she whispers. "I was up. You are always talking in your sleep," she adds carefully. "What do you dream?"

The atmosphere in the room grows still. We haven't really been friendly, but why not at least talk? So I laugh and decide to tell her my dream about my father slicing up his thigh. Her look of spell-bound consternation when she hears it makes me want to tell her more—so I tell her the one about my head being a page on a calendar. I even tell her the dream I had when I was a kid and was sure a periscope with the eye was chasing me, whether it was a dream or just something I had made up.

"Oh . . . oh . . . oh . . ." is all she can say.

I know she's never met anyone like me, same as I've never met anyone like her—but at least I was aware that people like her existed (in magazines, anyway). Suddenly I want her to see me, and I tell her about the pharmacist who tried to seduce me by offering me free crayons, of my sister trying to take me to the police station after my father beat me, and about Cousin Eddie's mom digging for gold in her Brooklyn basement.

"Gold . . . ? In the basement . . . ?"

No memory is too traumatic, personal, or stupid to relate, and I never feel ashamed or angry while telling them because they become stories that happened to someone else. I even embroider them.

"She did find something interesting."

"What?"

"Some ancient-looking Hebrew books. Could've been worth a fortune. But she burned them."

"Why?"

"Fear of spirits . . ."

I continue telling her my stories and meanly enjoy shocking her out of the safety and predictability of her world. There must be some good and sweet stories for me to tell as well, but I cannot think of them.

Eventually I find solid ground in Jewel Walker's movement class, where we mime walking miles by standing in one place, or are pulled by dogs that aren't there, or scale walls where there is no wall. I hold on to these lessons as a reason to stay in school and they help me get through visits home.

It's Christmas Eve by the wetlands. Ma and I wait for the phone to ring to see what's doing—but it doesn't. We have never had to wait by the phone before. Relatives and friends would just appear, as if they snatched a message to show up out of the air. The family is too spread out to have Christmases like we used to. Uncle Eddie is in another part of the Bronx. Uncle Frank and Iris are completely involved with Carmen (relieved to have done her duty) and Manny, who have two children now, a boy and a girl. Another reason we don't *parranda* around from house to house singing *aguinaldos* anymore is that it's hard to drag around the amplifiers my father now insists on using.

My brothers have made friends with neighborhood boys so they have gone to prowl the swamp in front of us. The plastic Christmas tree we now put up chimes Christmas carols. Ma checks on the *pernil*—and sings along with the tree: *"We three kings of Orient are . . ."* Even the pork shoulder in the oven looks lonely. The singing tree gets on my nerves and I unplug it.

"¿Qué pasa?" says Ma from the kitchen. "No Christmas spirit? It ain't like the old days, is it?"

She's right. I want the old days. Besides, I can sing one *aguinaldo* now—maybe I could've sung with my uncles . . .

"Take this bread pudding to Maya." She hands me the bread pudding and I take it down the block to our crazy Cuban neighbor. As I approach I hear her yelling to her son, *"¡Tú eres un drogadicto!"* So I'm quick with my delivery; I've heard her call her son a junkie before.

"Felicidades," I say, leaving it right on the coffee table nearest the door.

On my way back home I see my father coming toward me. From the lilt in his posture I can tell he's had a few—but what the hell, it's Christmas.

"Hey, Pops," I say cheerfully. "Ready for Christmas?"

He focuses for a moment, then flares up like a hot coal in a sudden wind.

"Who do you think you are, talking to me like that?"

What? Huh?

My eyes burn and I walk past him and into the house. He follows me and I think if I had delivered the rice pudding just ten minutes before or after I would've avoided him but I didn't and he corners me at the kitchen, yelling and screaming about who should've done this or that. There is a box of Cheerios on the table, and looking at the image of a bowl of cereal I imagine myself swimming in the milk, cavorting with a Cheerio as if it were an inner tube. Only my father's spittle spraying on my face brings me back to reality, and I decide to look him right in the eye, frankly, the way a baby might look at you with an open and direct gaze when they see you on the train or bus. It seems to dissipate the projectile of his anger and I am happy that I have been able to disarm him. When he looks away I feel I have been set free and go on up to my room, but I don't feel like I've won anything. I only feel that I am so tired of this shit and I count the days until I can go back to school.

CHAPTER 7

Stages of Fear

S onia can play that part!" a director announces. "It'll be hilarious!"

I'm cast as the personification of Peace in a production of the ancient Greek antiwar play *Lysistrata*. Representing Peace as a half-naked stripper I wear a feathered helmet, leaf pasties, sandals, and am directed to bump and grind around the outer lip of a raked stage, then pose triumphantly upon reaching its pinnacle. Somebody gives me the great idea to oil my body. On opening night I bump and grind like I did at rehearsal, but when I get to my triumphant pose my legs start to tremble! What the hell . . . ! I sheepishly make it offstage after the curtain call.

"Oh my God!" screams one of the students with a real part as she looks down at a stain on her costume.

"What's this stain?" she continues to yell, staring down at her breast.

"It's everywhere!" screams someone else. A domino effect of tension ripples through the actors as they look down at their costumes in horror, making this more of a drama than anything that had just happened onstage.

"Oh my God! My gown is chiffon! It's ruined!"

"My helmet is stained!"

"My armor has a smudge on it!"

"My tunic is fucked!"

"Where did this shit come from?"

Then they all stare at me.

"You . . . !"

"That oil!"

"It's ruining everything!"

"Jesus Christ . . ." somebody mutters, "how irresponsible!"

I have left an oil stain on every person I brushed against. Though the comments are about me they direct them to each other and I feel myself getting hot and angry, unable to find an opening, a moment of silence, in which to defend myself. They do not feel my side of the story is even worth considering, and I feel dismissed and swatted away like so much nothing as they flounce into their dressing areas, I am sure, poisonously murmuring about me.

The next day I am called into the head of the Drama Department's office. Is he going to criticize me for wearing oil, too?

"Sonia, you must get over your nervousness onstage."

"My nervousness . . . ?"

"You were so nervous you were trembling."

Nervous? It wasn't my nerves . . . it was my muscles. Didn't he get that?

"By the time you got to your final position the boat had sailed!"

The boat had sailed . . . ? What boat? Oh my God, was there a reference to a boat in the play that I had missed? Wait a minute— wait a minute—a boat sailing away sounds like a good thing. Is he saying I did something good?

———

Jewel Walker casts me as Cherie, a sorry chanteuse in the play *Bus Stop*, and when Cherie sings "That Old Black Magic," Walker laughs so hard he must lie down across the theater seats, and I am thrilled to have had that effect on him. But the day he shows us a Charlie Chaplin movie is a day of complete clarity for me. That little silent-movie guy arrests me! Yes, he does. My God, he plays a poor little Jew in Nazi Germany! Is this supposed to be funny? It is! It's hilarious even as I worry what the Gestapo will do to the little barber. I even laugh when he plays Hitler himself! The movie is over, but I get it, and I want to understand more, and I become obsessed with the Little Tramp and the things he can physically do. I get up early and go to the movement studio to practice jumps, walking into walls, spins, tumbles, and pratfalls. Isolating my head from my chest, from my midsection, from my ass becomes a full-time job. I even practice floating my head imperceptibly on my neck. Wearing baggy pants I practically wish I could grow a mustache. I get a book on Chaplin and am buoyed by the fact that his childhood was even more miserable and poverty-stricken than my ma's, even worse maybe because *he* had to struggle in *cold* weather.

Back home that summer, floating on my discovery of Chaplin, I go see about a job. It's as a go-go dancer in the meatpacking district on Fourteenth Street on the Lower West Side, but that's not what I tell Ma. Since the hours are noon to four I get away with telling her I'm going for a job as a waitress.

Grabbing my Chaplin book, I show up at 11:00 a.m. The bar is long and dark with just a few patrons ogling a girl who is already dancing on the small platform. Right away I know I have brought the wrong clothes to dance in—she is wearing pasties and a sparkly bikini bottom; I'm wearing dance tights under my bell-bottom jeans. I look at her more closely. Her skin is pale, her hair is red and fluffy, but there is something wrong with her face. It takes me a moment to realize what it is—she's missing some teeth. The bartender tells me that I am to dance for twenty minutes at a time. When it's my turn, I take my pants off, neatly fold them, and put them at the edge of the stage, along with my Indian macramé bag and my biography of Charlie Chaplin, and I get up on the stage and wait for the music to begin. It doesn't.

"Ya gotta play your own music, sista," yells the bartender.

I get off the stage, expecting him to give me a few quarters.

"And ya gotta use your own money," he adds.

I pull a dollar out of my bag, exchange it for quarters, and then select some songs on the jukebox. At this point there are four or five butchers wearing bloody white aprons at the bar eating roast beef sandwiches. I dance for twenty minutes, imagining myself as Chaplin in *The Rink* and trying to come as close to the edge of the stage as possible without looking down at my feet. When my time is up I gather my things and head for the bathroom because I can't wait to get back to my Chaplin book. But I'm just getting settled when there is a knock on the door.

"Hey, you can't just sit in here on your break!"

It's the bartender.

"You have to sit at the bar!"

Huh? Well, okay—I think.

I sit at the bar when the bartender points to a man and tells me the guy wants to buy me a drink. Before I can say yes or no there is a drink in front of me. I taste it and it is weak tea. The man joins me. I put the Chaplin biography in the space between us as armor or as something we can talk about. He is young and blue-eyed and has a mustache he keeps pulling on, keeping his head tucked in at an angle. I wonder if the man's drink tastes like tea as well.

"Do you like Charlie Chaplin?" I say, holding up my book.

He pulls on his mustache but says nothing.

By this time toothless dancer and me are the only girls at the bar full of men. A guy who could be my father walks in. The toothless dancer flutters over to him, slaps him on the back and grins like they are old friends. This cues the bartender to pour them both a drink and I see that her drink comes out of the same container as mine.

"One more drink for everybody," Toothless announces suddenly.

"Yay!" the bar men cheer. The Latin man is red in the face and grinning. What seems like moments later there is another cheer and the bartender serves everybody even more drinks and us women even more weak tea.

It's time for me to dance again.

By the time I am off the platform at 3:00 p.m. the little man can barely stand, and I know he is totally broke because Toothless walks him to the door and slaps him on the back, good-bye. Soon after, everyone leaves and the bar is empty. It's time to go so I'm gathering my clothes at the end of the day when the toothless dancer approaches me.

"My name's Doreen . . ." She smiles.

"Hi . . ." I say. I've never met anyone like her so I am curious.

"You know, you can make a lot of money if you want . . ."

I want.

". . . I'm going uptown to see my agent. Want to come?"

I'm surprised she has an agent, so I go along with her uptown, to an old building in the low forties. It's the kind of building you'd never know was there unless you were looking for it, shabby inside with peeling paint on the walls. We take a rickety elevator to the fourth floor and her agent's office, which seems to double as a lingerie shop. There are sparkly bras and panties and pasties spilling out of boxes haphazardly all over the place. He sits at a desk from another century with a slimy cigar stuck in his mouth and the ten or twelve hairs left on his head creeping over from one ear to the other.

"Hey, Doreen," he sneers, his eyes brightening at the sight of her.

"This is my friend Sonia. She might like to work if you can get her . . ."

He eyes me. "Yeah, I can get her some work—with the right outfit . . ."

As he moves to get up I start to back out. When I reach the door I turn and tumble down the stairway and get away as fast as I can.

The next day I find a job frying french fries at Jack in the Box and talk the owner into letting me dress up as a clown to greet the customers.

CHAPTER 8

Black Power

There is talk of freedom everywhere, but who is free and who is not? I overhear this in the school cafeteria. "I feel sorry for my mother, who never had the chance to work."

And a bittersweet memory is aroused. I'm seven and sick and tired of having the only mother in the neighborhood who has a job.

"Hey, Ma, how come you work? Don't you want to stay home with us like other ma's?"

She gathered me up into her arms, pulling me on the bed. "Are you kidding? *AveMaríaPurísima*—I wish I could stay home with you kids . . . nothing would be better for me, but if I don't work we don't got enough money to live."

And now at school I have to listen to girls talk about feminism and how their mothers hadn't been allowed to live up to their potential. Please!

Seeing the girls at my table toying with their food tumbles me back to the Bronx once again, and Ma struggling to make eight sandwiches out of one can of tuna! Suddenly I need to be around other people more like me. Aretha Franklin comes to my immediate rescue and, draping myself over the jukebox, I play her songs over and over again.

But then I do one better. I eventually go with a Pittsburgh boy who is a student when not in jail for robbing someone. He takes me to Homewood, Pittsburgh's ghetto, where I feel more at home. Homewood is a ghetto like one I've never seen, with private houses, lawns, porches, and barbecue grills in the backyards.

I like his friends. One of them is a barber with a girlfriend and a brand-new baby. They live in a little house and it seems the whole neighborhood, from old ladies to little kids, adores this child because they all come by for a chance to hold little Nikki in the air and to look at her with love, love, love like she is a new Christ. But Nikki's mother, a girl around my age, is angry all the time, especially at the barber. I don't know why she's so mad at him—the barber seems so sweet; he smiles all the time when he's not dropping down tired from working two jobs. Between being a barber by day and driving a jitney cab by night I figure this guy hardly rests. Still, I watch the young mother seethe because he is not doing enough.

One night my boyfriend and I double-date with them. We meet in a bar and have peach brandies and milk, then go to my boyfriend's parents' house for dinner. I am surprised that his mother is a doctor and his father a lawyer. The world is upside down and mixed up when a doctor and lawyer give birth to a college student who becomes a jailbird because he likes to steal, isn't it? The mother serves us chicken, and even without seeing the packaging I know it's Kentucky Fried, which means she's putting on this dinner party under duress. Then I see that she is a little afraid of my boyfriend! Why is she afraid of her son? My boyfriend *does* seem a little crazy, but he tells me it's really an act to keep him from becoming someone's "boyfriend" in jail.

Right after dinner the poor barber falls asleep, making his already infuriated girlfriend become even more unhinged with outrage. What will be their way out?

I have one foot in Homewood and another foot in school, and I suddenly feel I must grow a third foot to keep in New York, where a bunch of young Puerto Ricans called the Young Lords had taken over a church right across the street from Grandmother's house. All this talk of freedom reminds me of them. They were militant, angry, and wanted to give out free breakfast to poor kids just like the Black Panthers did in California. They set garbage on fire. My brother-in-law, Bill, said they were stupid to mess up their own neighborhood even more than it already was, that they should've messed up a rich neighborhood. "Hoodlums," said my uncle Ángel. "Look what they've done to the neighborhood, like it wasn't dirty enough."

But what flourishes up in my mind is that these Young Lords also said we should be proud of being Puerto Rican. Did they mean my family, too? Should I be proud of having a father like mine? And am I supposed to like "machismo" and letting your husband throw coconuts at your head if he wants to?

I'm slipping and sliding among these three worlds when my jailbird/student from Homewood starts telling me what to do and how to dress. I tell him to go jump in the lake and drop dead and he gets mad enough to strike me, making me bounce against the fence we are standing near. As I rebound, that old white-hot fury washes over me and I strike back with force coming up from my toes and shooting through my arms to my fists to his face. The last things I see before I connect with his nose are his beautiful brown eyes widening in surprise.

When the world falls back into place and I see the fence and the walkway and other students instead of a curtain of red, he is walking me back to the dorm, glad to be rid of me, I think.

But I am left with anger. Anger becomes my companion, sitting up on my shoulder at all times, entering a room before I do.

The next day I skulk in to read the notices in the hall of the Drama Department and become annoyed that I have been assigned a show. Why am I annoyed? Didn't I come to this school to be an actress? Reading on, I see that I am to be in a show called *Godspell* and wonder what that word means, anyway. The show is to be developed by the cast. Aha! I knew it would be something like that. The reason I am in it is that it hasn't been created yet! Perfect—a part in a play that doesn't exist. I should've known.

Why couldn't I be cast in a play about life in America? I gloomily answer my own question. Because spics like me aren't part of "life in America," at least as far as I can tell. I can't be in plays like *Our Town* because we don't live in "Our Towns." We live in "Our Barrios"—secret neighborhoods no one knows about but us.

I decide to get a cup of coffee and listen to Aretha Franklin for a quick pick-me-up at the cafeteria, but a sudden cold rainstorm forces me into the student union. Doubly pissed now, because I'm cold and wet, I sit and glance at the television. Something on the screen startles me. It's a favorite actor, Burt Lancaster, old now, counting from one to ten as the numbers flash over his head. Then there is a zany animation scored with a song sung by a rock-and-roll voice I can't quite place. I stay and watch until adorable actor James Earl Jones appears and astounds me by reciting the alphabet in a deliberate manner as the letters flash over *his* head. I think I am watching a show that teaches lip-reading.

But I am really taken aback by the street scene depicted because it reminds me of every neighborhood I have ever lived in.

And then a beautiful black couple appears. He is handsomeness personified with a mustache. She has a smile that goes on for miles.

I am amazed when I realize that in all the years I watched television in the South Bronx I hardly ever saw any people of color. But I am watching them now—on a show called *Sesame Street*.

CHAPTER 9

Godspell

First rehearsal of this unwritten show *Godspell*—five girls and five boys dressed as clowns act out Bible stories in a chain-link-fence enclosure—like a schoolyard. We all laugh and joke and the director directs nothing at all, except to tell us to act out the stories in any way we want to. I like screwing around onstage. Finally we force the lead clown, Jesus, onto a box, spread his arms out, and tie them to the fence with red ribbons. When our Jesus cries out, "Oh God, I'm busted," I zoom back in time to the Bronx, and sad-eyed cassock-wearing Father Fitzgerald and church, but I am struck that with all the religious instruction I suffered through, I had never heard any of these cool stories—except for one about Christ and Mary Magdalene, the whore. During rehearsal it becomes an exchange between a blues-playing musician and a flower child. The show needs some rock and roll and the director recruits a family of red-haired young brothers from his hometown who compose rock music with lyrics from hymns everyone has heard of but me.

My costume is a dress, a headband with a feather in it, and a fringed bra worn on the outside. On opening night I feel free and loose and happy to find a gag toy in my pocket put in by the costume designer. It's one of those party favors that makes a noise and unfurls as you blow into it. Looking around I notice that we all have gag toys in our pockets, which we find and improvise with on the spot during the show.

And with the final component in place—the audience—a miracle happens. They laugh at everything we do.

It's the end of our first performance. I'm at the back of the house with fellow actor Robin Lamont, a blonde girl always sweet, nice, and somehow true. She is usually dressed in a man's white T-shirt and raggedy jeans, but now, like me, she is dressed in a clown outfit. We look at each other and break into each other's arms, flabbergasted by the depth of feeling the show arouses in the audience and in us. My mind is flooded with ideas and connections—the harder the audience laughs, the more sorrow they will feel in the end! To register despair, make a joke about it!

Then it's great guns going full blast, four performances at the university, the director telling us he's taking the show to New York and who wants to come? I jump at the chance, Robin, too, and before we know it we are in a dirty little theater on the Lower East Side. New Carnegie Mellon alumni actors I sort of knew come on board. One of them is a beautiful girl with long red hair, whose confidence I envied the few times I came across her at school.

Rehearsal! Performance! Am I flying? I think I am! My feet aren't touching the ground—I must be flying! Wait—am I naked? Yes . . . no . . . I feel naked and bold even though I have clown clothes on. I look at the audience and think, hey—I dare you not to look at me, suckers!

After the last performance we hang around for a meeting with producers and composers and I register real-life drama unfolding before me: the director holding on to his partner's hands for security, and the disappointment in the faces of the actors who will be replaced. I know that I am part of the winning team, and though I don't know why, I am not surprised because I am not scared.

Old and new cast members come together in giving the new composer as difficult a time as possible. We want confusion onstage! Spontaneity and craziness is where it's at! We are even irritated by the producers' insistence on coming to rehearsals.

"Why couldn't they just wait until opening night to see the show, like everybody else?" our new Jesus quips.

I am given a sexy song that I get to sing straight to the audience. Just the kind of stuff I've been flirting with and doing in the show before real music was involved. But can I sing? No! But I can make believe I sing—so I do!

After rehearsals the cast visits Robin's parents' brownstone in Brooklyn Heights. I'm shocked at its beauty, with a recreation room on the first floor, a parlor with a baby grand piano on the second, living areas with beautiful sofas and chairs, a lovely patio, and even a terrace off her parents' room. I have never seen such luxury, not even at my father's old boss's house. We all hang out there, even sleep over sometimes, and one day I wait for Robin to come out of the shower and I look at the way she is dressed—white man's T-shirt, army surplus jeans, homemade macramé belt, cheap fabric old lady sandals, just the way she dresses at school.

"How come you didn't tell me you were rich, Robin?"

"Huh?" She laughs and proceeds to dry her long blonde hair by flipping her head back and forth so violently I think I hear her brains rattle. The cast becomes inseparable at her house and many move in while we rehearse, but how do I tell my parents I want to join them?

"I'm doing a show," I casually mention to Ma.

"*¿Qué, qué?*" my mother asks.

"It's part of the schoolwork I do . . ."

"*Pero*, are you going back to school?"

"I don't have to be in Pittsburgh to be in school. This is part of my schoolwork. They are going to pass me anyway."

"Oh . . ."

Then to my father.

"I'm going to stay downtown with some friends . . ."

"*¿Qué?*"

"To be much closer to my job . . ."

"Oh . . ."

"I'll be safer . . ."

"*Ajá* . . ."

And it's as easy as that. I could've told them I was going to keep house for seven dwarfs and they'd say, "Okay." And why wouldn't they, really? I'm high on rehearsals and want to leave my family behind with their boring problems. Forget them—I couldn't share the *Godspell* experience with them any more than I could smoke a joint with my grandmother.

I feel high as hell without drugs in rehearsals, in a mental state I have never been in before. Keyed up, poised, and alert for something to happen, though I don't even know what it is. I receive information like a plant, by osmosis. I make unconscious connections between choreography, harmonies, and gags. My mind is full of every thought I ever had, though specifically I think of nothing. I find ways to do things in rehearsals while I wonder how I ever came to those solutions. They just seem to happen naturally. In the evenings my mind is full of unarticulated questions. I am exhausted.

"Sonia . . ." It's Robin calling out to me in disbelief one night during dinner, as I plummet into sleep with a ham sandwich in my mouth. But I have to sleep quickly and hard so I can sort out ideas while I dream. I begin to know when notions become intuitively clear, and the best way to perform something makes itself known to me through no efforts of my own.

Every night, entering from the back of the theater, I sing in a sexy, syrupy Mae West way. A man looks in his program so I get right in his face and say, "It ain't in ya program . . ." I see a priest and say, "Ya colla's on backwards, Fadah," and I find it perversely satisfying when, just for a moment, he actually moves to adjust it. I love to rip the covers off people and put them on the spot.

I expand my part during the run. Suddenly I'm peeling down my sweat socks as if they are stockings, or straddling the edge of the cyclone fence, and shimmying up and down the end of it like a stripper on a curtain.

My mother, sister, and brothers come to see *Godspell* at least once, not like Robin's parents and their friends who come several times a week. But the theater is very foreign and expensive and difficult for my family, and the story of Jesus Christ told by clowns is too weird for Ma to bear, and besides it makes me uncomfortable that I am happy to see their backs as they make their way to the train after a performance.

Little Eddie comes to the show. His face is eager, his eyes owlish in aviator glasses and masses of curl sprouting from his head, and I remember the arguments he and his dad got into because of the length of his hair. But why is he still living at home? Doesn't he want to fly high and get away from the family, like me? I give a great performance that night.

"You sang flat!" he teases.

"I did not!

"You did, too! You telling me?"

Though he should know—by this time he is an accomplished musician, a professional, playing with greats like Mongo Santamaría and Gato Barbieri. I don't know if I sang flat or not, but I think I was good, and I know he thought so, too. But how can I share more with him? He is part of the old world I want to get away from—his loyalty to his mother, Bon Bon, and his physical closeness to home proves that.

I don't detain him when he comes because I am extra eager to return to visiting bars, then later to Robin's house with all the cast, to drink Constant Comment tea and smoke and listen to music. Besides, who cares about anything that happened before *Godspell*? Not me. Ha-ha! I have freed myself to do whatever I want to do—the show is successful, I am successful, and I don't need anybody to tell me so.

Curtain calls are not set. Actors take them or not as they wish and I am so spent after each show I never take a bow. One night the beautiful fellow actress with the long red hair I have always envied calls me out about it in front of others. "It is the responsibility of a performer to take a curtain call!" she says.

Devil anger on my shoulder sees this as an opportunity to awaken and thrive. Before I know it, it has dug its long, sharp claws into my back and is pushing me forward to attack. White flashbulbs explode in my head and I scream, "Fuck you, you tight-ass bitch!"

"You just don't know any better, and you are not professional!" she retorts.

My head reels as I sputter, "Fuck you!"

I am split and terrified that I can watch my horrible behavior, as if hovering above it all, yet cannot do anything to stop it. This new anger sticks to me like napalm and burns through my skin for days and days.

Later, onstage, during a song she tries to smile at me and make up, but when I try to smile back, fresh anger pulls me down under. This simmering rage becomes my state of being. Even one of the producers picks up on it.

"Would it kill you to smile?" he says to me on more than one occasion. I am even impatient when I am singled out to be interviewed, and when the newspaper reporter asks me if I ever feel in danger I answer sullenly, "Yeah, every time I go home for dinner."

CHAPTER 10

Unhappy Ending

When the show moves to a steady run in another theater it's time for the cast to clear out of Robin's house and get places of our own. I find a one-bedroom apartment on West Eighty-First Street. As I shop for Constant Comment tea and wheat germ and yogurt and Brie cheese and all the other new foods I was introduced to at Robin's house I think of Vanessa and wonder what she is doing besides having had a baby girl, who I'm sure looked just like her, the way she looked just like her mother and grandmother. With them it's like no man had anything to do with their existence, as if they were born from each other. Vanessa is probably doing to her daughter whatever her mother did to her. I don't want to see that. My life, though only twenty minutes from the Bronx on the subway, seems centuries away. Still—this apartment would've been the perfect place for us and I can't help feeling sorry it didn't happen.

One night after the show an agent leaves his card for me backstage. I call and go see him, not knowing what to expect. He's a nice enough man who tells me I need résumé shots.

"What's that?" I ask him.

"Standard actor's pictures. Head shots."

He gives me the name of a photographer, and the night before the shoot I wonder who I should be in the picture. I'm sure my hair will tell the world who and what I am. If it's natural I will be looked upon like a black person, if I straighten it I will be looked upon as a . . . what? I leave it natural and even forgo makeup on the day of the photo shoot, but all I end up looking like is a fourteen-year-old girl.

That night, I watch a girl in the show who always had a vision of what she wanted. She did summer stock, and showcases, and all the rest, always having a goal she ran to. I never ran *to* anything—I only ran away from things—and now I am stopped short, looking around and trying to figure out how I got here.

I give the photos to the agent but hope he never calls, but he does and I go on auditions, which I begin to hate more than anything. It's impossible for me to do at an audition what I do on the stage at night.

Producers and directors often want me to have a Puerto Rican accent, and though I can do it with my family it embarrasses me to do it in public. Or, I go up for parts of smart-talking black girls when *real* smart-talking black girls are much better at it than me. Why can't I just be myself? Besides, is this what I want? To run around in front of people, thinking, *Pick me, pick me,* so I can feel bad when they don't pick me even though I'm not sure I want to be picked in the first place? I don't know what to do. What have I gotten myself into? Months pass and I never get the jobs and feel I have let the agent down.

Then it's Christmas again and I busy myself with decorating my tree in my new apartment, but I get a yen for seeing all the decorations I made stories about long ago in the Bronx, so I go home for Christmas Eve. My sister and her husband, Bill, come, too. We eat and when it starts to get late and my father isn't home yet we wait for the violence, then are inexplicably surprised when it happens. Pops comes home like he's fallen to earth from another planet. His clothes are dirty because he went straight to drinking from working, and when his eyes don't focus I know he does not recognize us—again.

Swiftly, he runs into the kitchen, spewing incoherent words of hate about something that possibly happened twenty or so years ago when he and Ma lived on First Avenue. Finding his target, my mother, he manages to rip the phone off the wall and strike her on the head with it.

We subdue him somehow . . . maybe Bill does, but I snap to a halt and it occurs to me that in all the years of living through this I've never understood what he is hating about. With that thought I separate from the group and feel like I'm floating above them, in the same way I imagined my mother's mother, Encarnación Falcon, floating above her dead children in 1926 Puerto Rico. I look down on my family, thinking, *This will not go on anymore*. I am not a kid, I'm twenty years old, I've been to college, and I've got a job in a real off-Broadway show that people pay real money to see. I have even been mentioned in the newspaper. *This cannot go on*. I trudge up five blocks through the snow to find a pay phone and call the police, then trudge back to wait for them, not being sure of what they'll do but sure that if *I* don't do something I will lose my mother—if not that day, then on some other day when I am not there to protect her, because eventually one of his blows will hit her in exactly the spot that will end her life and the next day he won't even know what happened. Of this I am sure.

The police come as Joe and Petey and I gather the Christmas presents and call a cab that will take us all to my apartment in Manhattan.

There we sit and sourly open our presents on that sorry Christmas night. "Merry Christmas" we say to each other but our words are hollow, and I continually look at my mother and wonder about her. How can we share jokes and songs and stories and gossip and she not see that violence has been the driving force behind every decision we have ever made? How can I cherish the approval and warm hands on my face of someone who has let our situation go so far down the road to badness? I see her whole person but with a deep black hole in her center I cannot understand.

The *Godspell* people are the only ones I know to turn to. I know there are lawyers involved in show business and my mother needs one.

"We are not the kind of lawyers that your mother needs," they tell me carefully. "We do show business law."

"What's the difference?" *A lawyer is a lawyer,* I think.

"She needs a divorce lawyer. We can find one for you."

They find me a divorce lawyer and I am like a crusader, a woman with a mission, one single force driving me—the separation of my parents. The only time I veer off my goal is when I am onstage at night. There I am someone else with all the power in the world and I reign supreme. But off the stage I push my mother. My father won't vacate the house so I push my mother and brothers to find an apartment. They locate one in an unwelcoming Italian neighborhood. "Only for a while, Ma," I tell her. "The judge will give you the house." I ignore that she looks awful, even worse than when she was struck by Pops. His blows mar and hurt her skin and bones; the pain she has now radiates from her insides, blinding me. I push away any thoughts that I have caused this pain, but a part of me doesn't understand why she isn't elated. Happy. Like those women on the *Queen for a Day* television show when they get a washer/dryer, happy that their years of misery have paid off. Even as she continues to be immobile, numbed into robotic, passive submission, I push forward my plan to save her.

"I don't think your mother wants to go through with this," the lawyer confides in me, but the words bounce off like water on a new raincoat. I cannot stop myself any more than I can stop an avalanche or a bullet with my hand. This is my mission—if not, what did any of it mean? Living happily ever after is always the correct ending.

In court my mother and father sit apart, each with their respective lawyers, but I feel like the odd man out, that they are a team against me!

"With the telephone . . . ?" the judge asks.

"Yes," I say. "He hit her with the telephone." My testimony is short and quick, and I feel so much like the little girl I was sitting in the big chair at my father's boss's house so long ago I have to remind myself that I am not little anymore. Still, suddenly I look down at my clothes. My God, did I forget to take off my *Godspell* costume? Am I wearing a clown outfit in court? No! I'm not—I am wearing the proper clothes of a grown-up person and I find comfort in that fact as the judge pronounces my parents divorced. That's when I see my father stumble like he's been hit hard, and I think I see my mother's heart go out to him.

"Ma, we did it!" I say when it's over outside the courtroom. But she looks away from me, not happy and grateful like I thought she'd be. Months pass and she does nothing to retain the wetlands house, and my brothers get beat up by the Italian kids in the neighborhood they now live in, though I push and push and push, through the rest of the winter and into the spring.

That June I am in a photo shoot for the *New York Times* newspaper. I pose with my finger cymbals. The Sunday after, there is an article about up-and-coming Broadway stars and I am one of them—I think I am happy but honestly don't know how important or serious it is. What can I compare it to? Is it as important as Ma's divorce or her safety or the loss of her house . . . ? I push . . .

"You'll go to court and get the house you've worked so hard for, Ma."

But months pass and my mother and brothers continue to live in a rental while my father occupies the house, so I visit and try to push *him*. I find it strange that he is not angry with me.

"What the hell—life happens," he says.

"You have to move out, Pops, so Ma can live here. It's the right thing to do."

"I am not going to move."

"Then sell it and split the money. If you don't the judge will sell it for you for less than what it's worth—"

He cuts me off. "Look," he says. "I don't care about the house. I never cared about the house. That was your mother's thing, your mother wanting to do whatever she wanted."

I am ashamed that he is petty and won't do the manly thing that I am sure my uncle Eddie or uncle Frank would do in the same situation. But I push for a decent and good solution even as spring drags into summer.

When I don't push I do the show at night, hope I don't have any auditions, and fool around decorating my apartment. Now, I've decided to draw a roundabout arrow on a wall that will eventually point to a light switch. The arrow will come up from nowhere on the floor and turn in on itself until it finds its destination. Taking a break, I make myself a cup of Constant Comment as a reminder of my new life and the control I have over it, when the phone rings. It is my uncle Félix in Puerto Rico. He talks of going on a Disney Cruise and somehow ending up in New York for a short visit. We laugh as we struggle with our languages until talk of vacations makes him mention that my parents recently found time to vacation together in Puerto Rico.

I am knocked solid.

"*¿Qué pasa?*" he asks.

I try to answer but the swig of tea I have just taken shoots out of my nose.

"*Nada,*" I gasp, choking and coughing. "Nothing . . . something just went down wrong . . . I'll be okay in a *momento.*" In that *momento* all the anxiety that I've been trying to contain for months bursts out in a laugh.

"What's so funny?" asks my uncle in Spanish.

"Nothing," I gasp. But I really mean everything. Everything is funny. It's just all too funny for me. I say my good-byes, hang up the phone, and look at the pointless arrow on my wall, and suddenly the fact that it's perfect and hell-bent on going nowhere really makes me laugh; and I laugh because of what I am finally sure about.

That I know nothing, nothing, nothing.

CHAPTER 11

The Beginning

What do I love? What do I love? I must get back to something I love outside of myself or drown, so I go to Clark Center and take a 10:00 a.m. acrobatics class, an 11:00 a.m. jazz class, a 1:00 p.m. ballet class, every day before doing the show at night. Keep moving, keep moving, a moving target is harder to hit, I tell myself. And in all this hiding in plain sight I get a message from my answering service to call my agent and I cringe. What now? How come the agent hasn't figured out that I know nothing? Doesn't he feel disappointed that I never get any of the jobs he sends me up for? Can't he tell I don't understand a thing? Apparently not, because he wants me to audition for *Sesame Street*.

The green-and-white empire-waist dress I decide on wearing is comfortable and fits me perfectly. I love it because Ma made it for me from some material sent to her from Puerto Rico. Cheap Indian sandals reveal big toes I decide to show off as an act of defiance. My hair is natural and long because I don't care what people think I am.

I go to the Children's Television Workshop on Broadway and Sixty-Third Street, where I am to meet *Sesame Street*'s executive producer, Jon Stone. My big feet enter the room before I do. It's just him in his office, no conference room with chairs pushed against the wall.

He is a big man with curly white hair and a beard with a pencil stuck through it. Very friendly with cherubic lips, but I can't help seeing a storm brewing behind his eyes and brow.

There is a board with a black circle, a circle with stripes on it, a black square, and a square with stripes on it. After we chat he asks me to make believe he is a four-year-old, and that I should explain which two items on the board are the same. I realize there are two right answers and we laugh about that, and I like that things aren't cut-and-dried, and I notice he has several wayward, wiry, rogue eyebrow hairs sticking out.

Then he asks me to tell a scary story, once again to him, as if *he* were a little kid. Without thinking I quickly and immediately go back to Third Avenue where I was most scared. The dream or experience I had with the periscope with a big eye watching, stalking my every move and breathing down my neck, jumps into my mind.

"Once upon a time in the olden days there lived a little girl who lived alone in a woods full of goblins and fairies and monsters," I begin. "She had to hunt for her food every day and one day out hunting she felt something watching her. She turned around but couldn't see what it was, but she couldn't shake the feeling of long hairs sweeping along her neck. It made her feel so creepy and nervous she couldn't catch a thing to eat. I mean—who could hunt in a situation like that? This went on for days until she got very hungry."

Jon Stone looks amused but would still like me to get on with it.

"Finally she had had enough and she yelled, 'Why don't you come out and look me in the eye?' And it did. *It* was a big, ugly eye that had been watching her all the time! It was huge and bloodshot and had long sticky eyelashes that practically swept across the back of her neck. It scared her so much she ran, and ran, but the eye got closer and closer. Finally it got so close the little girl had no choice but to face it. She had no weapons, so she decided to bite it."

I wait for a reaction from Jon. His bushy eyebrows flicker for one instant. I go on.

"Once she had done that she figured, what the hell, I might as well eat it. I'm hungry anyway. She did, and it was disgusting. Crunchy on the outside and soft on the inside—like eating a soft-boiled egg with the shell on! Yuck!"

This makes Jon smile. I am encouraged and continue.

"But she was brave and sucked it up anyway. She walked back to her cave feeling sick to her stomach. But she was glad she ate the eye even though it tasted lousy and made her want to throw up."

For one second I don't know where this story is going—but I plunge on.

"And the next day, when she woke up, she noticed something funny had happed. She wasn't afraid anymore. Not only that—the sky was really blue, and the sun was clear and bright, and the flowers prettier. So eating the eye not only made her not afraid and filled her tummy, it also made her see things better. The End."

He looks pleased. I am glad to have found a use for that story. I think I wouldn't mind auditioning for things if I could always make up my own material. Who wouldn't? Jon looks at me for a moment, we say good-bye, and he sends me on my way.

That's it? I think as I get on the elevator. Then I go home, because there is nothing else to do but wait for the next thing to happen.

Acknowledgments

It "takes a village" to make a book, so let me thank my agent, Jennifer Lyons, for her unwavering support and enthusiasm in finding the right publisher, and Andrea Davis Pinkney, my editor at Scholastic, for her encouragement and vision and for allowing me to write freely while guiding me through the process.

Gracias to copy editor Monique Vescia for smoothing the words, and to Elizabeth Parisi for creatively presenting the best visual introduction to the book possible.

I've changed the names of my friends to protect their privacy. However, any names of *Godspell* cast mentioned in this memoir are their own, as are the names of my relatives and siblings. A special thanks goes out to my siblings for willingly traveling to the past with me. Thanks to my daughter, Gabriela Rose Reagan, for her sweet, supportive presence. And finally, an extra-special thanks goes to my husband, Richard Reagan, for patiently listening, critiquing, and graciously giving feedback for each and every draft.

Memories can be both elusive and concrete. When I look at early footage of myself on television, I sometimes cannot remember taping the segments, but I do remember what I think is more important: what my feelings were at that time in my life—if I was angry, happy, or sad, in or out of love.

On the other hand, and maybe because there are only a few black-and-white photos of me as a kid, remembering the past events in this memoir often took on a magical quality. I'm sure I remember occurrences I couldn't possibly have known about because I was simply too young. I was positive parties happened in one apartment only to discover, after chatting with relatives, that the gathering had happened in another, and remembering family situations with my siblings was cause for both sadness and hilarity as we recollected the same events differently.

So if I've learned anything from writing this memoir, it is mostly this: Though lives are made up of real events as sure as a television taping or a black-and-white photo, lives are more often shaped and colored by how we remember those events and the series of feelings that went along with them.

About the Author

Sonia Manzano is the actress who defined the role of Maria on the acclaimed television series *Sesame Street*. She has won fifteen Emmy Awards for her television writing and was twice nominated for an Emmy Award as best performer in a children's series. Sonia is the author of the Pura Belpré Honor Book *The Revolution of Evelyn Serrano*, hailed in starred reviews by *Kirkus Reviews* as "stunning" and in *Booklist* as a "wry . . . moving" novel. The book was also cited by *Kirkus Reviews* as a Best Children's Book of 2012. Adding to Sonia's credits, *People en Español* magazine named her one of America's most influential Hispanics, and she has been recognized by the Congressional Hispanic Caucus in Washington, D.C. Sonia holds an honorary doctorate in fine arts from the University of Notre Dame. She lives in New York City with her husband.